W9-DIF-345

MOVIE TREASURES OF THE '40s & '50s

Gynnath Ford

Highlands Publishing

Nashville, Tennessee

Published by:
Highlands Publishing
Box 50021
Nashville, TN 37205

ISBN: 0-9676496-4-1

Editor: Gail M. Kearns, GMK Editorial Services, Santa Barbara, California
Cover Design: Robert Howard, Robert Howard Graphic Design, Fort Collins, Colorado
Interior Book Design: Christine Nolt, Cirrus Design, Santa Barbara, California

Printed in the United States of America

*To parents, grandparents, and other
noble men and women who contributed to this
country's well-being during the '40s and '50s
and often became the inspiration
for the movies made during these eras.*

Table of Contents

Acknowledgment

I am very grateful to the various individuals who helped to make this book project a success.

Thanks to my editor, Gail Kearns, for her fine editing skills and suggestions, which brought the manuscript to fruition.

To my mentor, Dan Poynter of Para Publishing, who knows the value of a good team, and steered me in the right direction.

To Robert Howard of Graphic Design for his beautiful cover design.

To Christine Nolt of Cirrus Design for her artistic interior layout.

And to my faithful wife and advisor, Ruth Ford of Ford Enterprises (also my movie companion), to whom I am deeply indebted.

Introduction

I was a teenager in the 1940s, and then got married to my childhood sweetheart in the '50s. I have three vivid remembrances of those times. My first memory is of Saturday afternoon matinees, where I sat in a balcony separated by an aisle from the blacks who were allotted a very small section in the theater. Then there were the photos in the local bank window of servicemen in the armed forces, some with a star denoting they had died in action. Finally, there was the advent of television.

I was an avid moviegoer. Looking back, I realize I had no idea what an impact the movies were having on me. I just knew I couldn't see enough of them. During this twenty-year span, films pertaining to the Second World War were prominent. *Mrs. Miniver* and *Sergeant York* made quite an impression on me, especially since Alvin York was from my home state of Tennessee. Race-related movies like *The Defiant Ones, Blackboard Jungle, Pinky,* and *Imitation of Life* helped me to develop more compassion for people of color. In my teens, with the appearance of television, late night movies became a favorite pastime of mine.

During these years, movie theater attendance declined, for a variety of reasons: men were off at war and women were working; people's lifestyles changed after the war; there was the obvious comfort of viewing TV in the home. At first, the motion picture industry forbade their employees to watch this new media, but it didn't take long before it accepted the challenge and began to make bigger and better films. TV was good for movies, and movies were good for TV.

Now, of course, we have video, and you have the opportunity to see many of the wonderful films made during these decades by going to your local video store or library, which brings me to the purpose of this book.

In this volume, I have selected 100 of my favorite films of the '40s and '50s. Eleven of these movies were reviewed in my first book, *Treasures of the Silver Screen,* and an asterisk in the table of contents notes them. After I had made my picks, I realized I couldn't go to press without recommending the following films, also reviewed in my previous book.

An Affair to Remember (1957)
Bad Day at Black Rock (1955)
Bridge on the River Kwai (1957)
The Caine Mutiny (1954)
The Defiant Ones (1958)
From Here to Eternity (1953)
High Noon (1952)
How Green Was My Valley (1941)
The Man Who Knew Too Much (1956)
Mrs. Miniver (1942)
Notorious (1946)
On the Waterfront (1954)
The Paradine Case (1948)
Pride of the Yankees (1942)
Red River (1948)
Singin' in the Rain (1952)
The Thing from Another World (1951)
The Treasure of the Sierra Madre (1948)
Twelve Angry Men (1957)
Witness for the Prosecution (1957)

All of these movies are the promise of an eventful couple of hours of entertainment where I hope you, too, will capture optimism of the times when I first began to attend the cinema in small-town America. People in their retirement age can recapture their youth, middle-aged viewers will be enthralled with their roots, and youngsters can experience the spirit that has given us much of today's prosperity. There is something for everyone in *Movie Treasures of the '40s & '50s*. Happy viewing!

Gynnath Ford

The African Queen
Adventure/Romance 1951

Director: John Huston

Starring: Humphrey Bogart, Katharine Hepburn, Robert Morley

• •

STORY CONCEPT—A hard-drinking riverboat captain and a prim missionary spinster motor down a treacherous African river to escape German troops during World War I. Despite their differences and constant quarrels, they eventually discover a few things about themselves from each other.

THEME—People learn to love and appreciate one another more when they have a common goal.

FAVORITE SCENE—Rose Sayers (Hepburn) is transformed when she experiences the thrill of conquering the river rapids. Captain Allnut (Bogart) celebrates the victory by getting drunk, whereupon Rose pours all of his booze in the river.

MEMORABLE LINES—Rose introduces the idea to sabotage a German ship by torpedoing it.

Charlie: We can't do that!
Rose: How do you know? You never tried it.
Charlie: Well, yeah, but I never tried shooting myself in the head neither.

TAKE NOTE—Much of the humor was absent in the original novel and in the film script. It evolved through Bogart's and Hepburn's ad-libbing. Director Huston kept it in. Also, since Huston insisted on realism, the leeches on Bogart were real.

TRIVIA QUIZ—What is the name of Charlie's boat in the movie? (Answer No. 1)

Imagination is the highest kite one can fly. —LAUREN BACALL

Behold the turtle. He makes progress only when he sticks his neck out. —JAMES BRYANT CONANT

All That Heaven Allows
Romance 1955

Director: Douglas Sirk

Starring: Jane Wyman, Rock Hudson, Agnes Moorehead, Gloria Talbot, William Reynolds

● ●

STORY CONCEPT—A prosperous New England widow falls in love with one of her gardeners. Her children and country club friends disapprove heartily because he is younger and far beneath her social status.

THEME—True love rises above petty prejudices.

FAVORITE SCENE—Cary Scott (Wyman) has sacrificed everything, including her new love, Ron Kirby (Hudson), for her children. Then she finds out that they have plans for their own lives, which do not include her. Her daughter, Kay (Talbot), announces that she's getting married, and her son, Ned (Reynolds), says he plans to study abroad.

MEMORABLE LINES—Kay rambles on about life and aging with her mother.

Kay: In Egypt, a widow used to be sealed in her husband's tomb. Of course that doesn't happen anymore.
Cary: Doesn't it?

TAKE NOTE—The three stars—Wyman, Hudson, and Moorehead —and Director Sirk, are reunited after the success of *Magnificent Obsession*, the movie that made Hudson, a former truck driver, a star.

TRIVIA QUIZ—What kind of bird is Ron hunting in the snow when he falls from a cliff? (Answer No. 2)

The mass of men lead lives of quiet desperation.

—HENRY DAVID THOREAU

Anatomy of a Murder
Drama 1959

Director: Otto Preminger

Starring: James Stewart, Lee Remick, Ben Gazzara, Arthur O'Connell, George C. Scott, Kathryn Grant Crosby

● ●

STORY CONCEPT—A small-town lawyer is hired to defend an army officer accused of murder. He faces a double challenge—the lack of cooperation from his defendant and a talented big-city prosecutor.

THEME—Suspicion and anger are twins that can get you in double trouble.

FAVORITE SCENE—Claude C. Dancer (Scott), prosecuting attorney, interrogates witness Mary Pilant (Crosby), alleged mistress of the victim, and is shocked to find that she is the victim's daughter. This is a turning point in the trial.

MEMORABLE LINES—Judge Weaver (Welch) to the courtroom when a request is made for a dog to appear in court: "A creature that cannot talk would be a welcome relief."

TAKE NOTE—The book by the same name was written by Robert Traver, Justice of Michigan Supreme Court. It was on the best-seller list for 61 consecutive months. Joseph Welch, who plays Judge Weaver, was a famous Boston lawyer who later became a judge.

TRIVIA QUIZ—A two-word phrase was tossed around freely during the defense scenes of Lieutenant Manion (Gazzara). It also got a chuckle in the closing scene. What is it? (Answer No. 3)

Suspicion is about the only thing that can feed on itself and grow larger all the while. —ANONYMOUS

A beautiful woman lacking discretion and modesty is like a fine gold ring in a pig's snout. —THE BIBLE

15

As Young As You Feel

Comedy 1951

Director: Harmon Jones

Starring: Monte Woolley, Constance Bennett, David Wayne,
Jean Peters, Marilyn Monroe, Albert Dekker,
Thelma Ritter

• •

STORY CONCEPT—In an effort to get his job back, a retired printer of a print shop boldly impersonates the president of the parent company and succeeds in changing the company's policy on retirement. What he didn't foresee is just the tip of the iceberg—his boss's wife wanting to divorce her husband and marry him.

THEME—A person may be retired, but that doesn't mean there is nothing left to achieve.

FAVORITE SCENE—John Hodges (Woolley) is shocked when the boss's wife, Lucille (Bennett), comes to his home to tell him that she is in love with him and she's leaving her husband.

MEMORABLE LINES—Hodges speaks with his prospective son-in-law, Elliott (Wayne), about going to the top to regain his job.

Elliott: Do you mean you'd go to Consolidated Motors?
Hodges: I'd seriously consider going to the North Pole by dog sled in the heart of winter if it would get my job back!

TAKE NOTE—Monte Wooley, the star of this movie, was a former Yale professor.

TRIVIA QUIZ—What made Lucille McKinley fall in love with the much older John Hodges? (Answer No. 4)

A great many people who are worried about adding years to their life should try adding life to their years. —ANONYMOUS

The Bad and the Beautiful
Drama 1952

Director: Vincent Minnelli

Starring: Kirk Douglas, Lana Turner, Walter Pidgeon,
Dick Powell, Barry Sullivan, Gloria Grahame,
Gilbert Roland

• •

STORY CONCEPT—A writer, a director, and an actress, all victims of a successful but ruthless film producer, tell their story of how they were exploited to a studio executive.

THEME—He who rises to great heights on the broken wings of others is destined for a great fall.

FAVORITE SCENE—After her first successful film, former alcoholic Georgia Lorrison (Turner) leaves the celebration party and goes to the home of her producer/director, Jonathan Shields (Douglas), with whom she's in love. She finds him with another woman and flees, heartbroken.

MEMORABLE LINES—In Georgia's unkempt apartment, Jonathan admires the memorabilia of her father, an actor, who also had a problem with alcohol.

Georgia: I hate him!
Jonathan: Make up your mind. You hate him but you've built a shrine to him. You can't be a star in a cemetery. (Pause) You're a bit player—not a star—until you get yourself out of this tomb.

TAKE NOTE—In this film, Lana Turner plays an actress who started as a movie extra. In her own career she began as a movie extra in *A Star Is Born*.

TRIVIA QUIZ—What brought the writer, director, and actress together? (Answer No. 5)

> *Consider how much more you often suffer from your anger and grief than from those very things for which you are angry and grieved.* —MARCUS AURELIUS

Battle Hymn

War/Drama 1957

Director: Douglas Sirk

Starring: Rock Hudson, Martha Hyer, Anna Kashfi,
Dan Duryea, Don DeFore, Philip Ahn

● ●

STORY CONCEPT—This is the true story of Dean Hess, a World War II pilot, who accidentally dropped a bomb on a German orphanage. He later starts an orphanage in Korea.

THEME—Out of tragedy come compassion and peace of mind.

FAVORITE SCENE—Colonel Hess (Hudson), a former minister, overcome with emotion, is unable to say a prayer at the gravesite of his young assistant, En Soon Yang (Anna Kashfi), who helped him establish the orphanage. An elderly Korean consoles him.

MEMORABLE LINES—Hess attempts to recruit an elderly Christian Korean storekeeper to assist with the children.

Hess: Matthew said, "Whosoever receives one of these little ones receives me."

Storekeeper: I will stay. My store was destroyed by fire. Helping these little ones is something that can never be destroyed.

TAKE NOTE—*Battle Hymn* won a Golden Globe for Best Film Promoting International Understanding.

TRIVIA QUIZ—What prompted Colonel Dean Hess to start an orphanage in Korea? (Answer No. 6)

> *Every child born into this world is a new thought of God, an ever-fresh and radiant possibility.* —KATE DOUGLAS WIGGIN

Ben-Hur

Drama 1959

Director: William Wyler

Starring: Charlton Heston, Stephen Boyd, Haya Harareet, Martha Scott, Sam Jaffe, Jack Hawkins, Hugh Griffith

STORY CONCEPT—Childhood friends become bitter enemies. One of them, a wealthy Jew, proves a threat to Roman rule so he's condemned to being a galley slave. Through the providence of God, he becomes a free man and gains revenge. His life is touched by Jesus of Nazareth, both as a slave and a free but troubled man.

THEME—Personal revenge does not satisfy the heart's deepest yearnings.

FAVORITE SCENE—Ben-Hur's (Heston) steward, Simonides (Jaffe), asks permission for his daughter, Esther (Harareet), to marry a nobleman. Ben-Hur is struck with her beauty and demeanor, and grants permission. Esther glances away when Ben-Hur stares at her. Then she lifts her eyes to meet his gaze.

MEMORABLE LINES—During a private interlude between Ben-Hur and Esther the night after permission is given for her to marry:

Ben-Hur: If you were not a bride, I would kiss you good-bye.
Esther: If I were not a bride, there would be no good-byes to be said. (She hands him a ring.) You will wear it until you meet the woman you marry?
Ben-Hur: Yes, until then. (They kiss and she departs.)

TAKE NOTE—The eleven-minute chariot race, which took three months to film, had very few shots with doubles. Boyd (Messala) was actually dragged behind the chariot.

TRIVIA QUIZ—What is unusual about the appearance of Jesus in the film? (Answer No. 7)

Every person should have a special cemetery lot in which they bury the faults of friends and loved ones. To forgive is to set a prisoner free and discover the prisoner was you. —ANONYMOUS

The Best Years of Our Lives
Drama 1946

Director: William Wyler

Starring: Myrna Loy, Fredric March, Dana Andrews, Teresa Wright, Virginia Mayo, Cathy O'Donnell, Harold Russell

● ●

STORY CONCEPT—Three veterans of World War II befriend each other on a flight home to their Midwestern town of Boone. Once back in civilian life, relationships with their wives and a girlfriend, and their jobs, present challenges that bring the three of them closer together and produce major lifestyle changes.

THEME—Freedom brings a high price and painful adjustments.

FAVORITE SCENE—Wilma (O'Donnell) confronts her fiancé, Homer (Russell), in his garage workshop. He's been avoiding her and she wants to know why. He takes her to his bedroom where he asks her to help him remove his artificial arms in preparation for bed. Homer feels he can't ask Wilma to marry him because he's a cripple, but his trying to shock her doesn't diminish her love for him.

MEMORABLE LINES—Al (March) talks to Fred (Andrews), who is married to a materialistic, two-timing wife, about his own wife and family: "We have an unusual relationship in our family. We tell each other things."

TAKE NOTE—World War II veteran Russell, who lost his hands in the war, is the only person to win two Oscars for the same role: Best Supporting Actor and a special Oscar "for bringing hope and courage to his fellow veterans through his appearance" in the movie. It was also his debut.

TRIVIA QUIZ—What made William Wyler such a great choice to direct this film? (Answer No. 8)

It's not the wrappings but the gift on the inside that counts.
—ROGER CRAWFORD

The Bishop's Wife

Comedy/Fantasy 1947

Director: Henry Koster

Starring: Cary Grant, Loretta Young, Gladys Cooper, David Niven, Monty Woolley

● ●

STORY CONCEPT—A bishop preoccupied with raising money to build a new church neglects his wife and children. An angel appears on the scene to help him get his priorities straight. His ignored wife becomes infatuated with the angel, which brings the bishop to his senses.

THEME—A person can be too heavenly minded to be of any earthly good.

FAVORITE SCENE—The angel, Dudley (Grant), becomes a big hit with the bishop's children when he tells them the story of David and the lion. The adults also listen, awestruck.

MEMORABLE LINES—Pessimistic Professor Wutheridge (Woolley) speaking to Dudley: "I was in love with a lady years ago. I never told her. She married an athlete. He was an oaf, who only finished the eighth grade, but he knew enough to say, 'I love you.'"

TAKE NOTE—This film was originally cast with David Niven as the angel and Cary Grant as the bishop. When Koster was brought in as a director, he felt that this was the wrong combination, so the two actors agreed to exchange parts. Both were unhappy with the change throughout the picture.

TRIVIA QUIZ—There was a remake of this film done in 1996. What was its title and who directed it? (Answer No. 9)

The average man does not know what to do with his life, yet wants another one which will last forever. —ANATOLE FRANCE

Blackboard Jungle

Drama 1955

Director: Richard Brooks

Starring: Glenn Ford, Sidney Poitier, Ann Francis, Richard Kiley, Vic Morrow, Louis Calhern, Margaret Hayes

• •

STORY CONCEPT—A returning Navy veteran begins a new career as a teacher in an all-boys vocational school. While dealing with his pregnant wife who fears losing her second child, he endures ridicule, slander, and a beating by some of his students. His tenacity and humanity enable him to reach many of the young boys.

THEME—Courage and sincerity impress neglected and misguided youth.

FAVORITE SCENE—Richard Dadier (Ford), a new teacher, listens to a lecture on prejudice and name-calling by the principal and realizes he is the accused. He is enraged to think that he's condemned without a hearing. His strong denial of the charges causes the principal to back off and apologize.

MEMORABLE LINES—Dadier comes home to his wife, Anne (Francis), after being severely beaten by hooligan students.

Anne: You're never going back to that school! Never!

Richard: Oh, yes I am! I'm beaten up but I'm not beaten! There's a difference. I'm not quitting.

TAKE NOTE—Sidney Poitier plays his first major role in this film. Twelve years later he portrays a teacher in *To Sir with Love*, featured in the book *Treasures of the Silver Screen*.

TRIVIA QUIZ—What is the theme song in this movie, which became a major rock hit? (Answer No. 10)

Not failure but low aim is crime. —JAMES RUSSELL LOWELL

Broken Arrow

Western/Romance 1950

Director: Delmer Daves

Starring: James Stewart, Jeff Chandler, Debra Paget,
Will Geer, Basil Rysdael

● ●

STORY CONCEPT—A former army officer saves the life of a wounded Apache boy and appoints himself U.S. ambassador to the tribe. He assists in the peace treaty between the Apaches and the U.S. who have been fighting for many years. He experiences love and tragedy during this time.

THEME—People who are different have the same basic needs: love, respect, and independence.

FAVORITE SCENE—Peacemaker Tom Jeffords (Stewart) marries Sonseeahray (Paget) whom he's met only twice. They say their vows, mix their blood, and ride off on white horses into the wilderness.

MEMORABLE LINES –The second time Jeffords visits the Apache camp, he looks for Sonseeahray and finds her at the stream.

Jeffords: My feet are tired from finding you accidentally. (Legend says that the only way Indian braves and maidens should meet before marriage is accidentally.)
Sonseeahray: I washed my hair twice and my clothes three times while waiting for you.

TAKE NOTE—The film depicts Indians as intelligent and worthy of respect. The day after the film finished shooting, Jimmy Stewart married Gloria McLean, his wife and companion for life.

TRIVIA QUIZ—What television role is Will Geer, who portrays Stewart's enemy, noted for? (Answer No. 11)

Ancestry is most important to those who have done nothing themselves. —LOUIS L'AMOUR

Broken Lance

Western/Romance 1954

Director: Edward Dmytryk

Starring: Spencer Tracy, Robert Wagner, Katy Jurado,
Jean Peters, Richard Widmark, E.G. Marshall,
Hugh O'Brien, Earl Holliman

● ●

STORY CONCEPT—A cattle baron in the Old West resists change and the new laws of the range.

THEME—Love has the power to overcome revenge.

FAVORITE SCENE—Cattle rancher Matt Devereaux (Tracy) is sued by the copper mine owners and brought to trial. His temper and his willingness to take the law into his own hands make his case weak, so his youngest son, Joe (Wagner), takes the blame for the attack on the miners and goes to prison for three years.

MEMORABLE LINES—During dinner, Matt and the governor's outspoken daughter, Barbara (Peters), discuss Matt's unwillingness to delegate authority to his sons.

Barbara: Why wouldn't you be willing to let one of them take over for you in town?
Matt: I think that Ben (Widmark) could take over in town.
Barbara: But you would lose control. (Pause) That would mean giving up part of the ranch to him.
Matt: Uh huh.
Barbara: And you wouldn't like that.
Matt: Uh huh. And what's more I'm not going to do it.

TAKE NOTE—Clark Gable, who was awed at Spencer Tracy's acting, said he was so good that nobody in the business could approach his talent.

TRIVIA QUIZ—How does Joe, who is half Comanche, end the strife with his half brothers? (Answer No. 12)

> *You can't make a place for yourself in the sun if you only live under the family tree.* —JOHN MASON

Call Northside 777

Drama/Biography 1948

Director: Henry Hathaway

Starring: James Stewart, Richard Conte, Lee J. Cobb, Helen Walker, Kasia Orzazewski

• •

STORY CONCEPT—A newspaper reporter reads an ad offering a $5000 reward for finding the killer of a police officer—a crime that took place twelve years earlier. His investigation leads him to a widow whose son was convicted of the crime. The case is reopened, the innocent son is released, and the killer is found. Based on a true story.

THEME—A relentless search for justice reveals truth, which sets an imprisoned man free.

FAVORITE SCENE—Frank Wiecek (Conte), the imprisoned son, asks reporter P.J. McNeal (Stewart) to call off the investigation because the publicity is upsetting to his family, who just wants their privacy.

MEMORABLE LINES—McNeal interviews Wiecek's mother (Orzazewski), who placed the reward ad in the paper.

Mrs. Wiecek: Eleven years I scrubbed floors and saved money.
McNeal: Eleven years. That's a long time.
Mrs. Wiecek: You just say it. My boy lived it. Eleven years I dream and I work.

TAKE NOTE—Wiecek was paid $1000 for the rights to this story. The state also compensated him $24,000 for false imprisonment.

TRIVIA QUIZ—Where does the title of this movie come from? (Answer No. 13)

> *The human spirit is stronger than anything that can happen to it.* —GEORGE C. SCOTT

Casablanca

Drama/Romance 1942

Director: Michael Curtiz

Starring: Humphrey Bogart, Ingrid Bergman, Claude Rains, Paul Henreid, Dooley Wilson

● ●

STORY CONCEPT—A callous nightclub owner at a wartime way station has his world turned upside down when his lost love returns with her freedom-fighting husband. The flame of love is ignited again, but there is a greater cause, greater than their personal feelings, which leads to a heart-rending decision.

THEME—Character takes first place over love.

FAVORITE SCENE—Ilsa (Bergman) asks Sam (Wilson), the nightclub piano player, to play "As Time Goes By" for old times sake. Rick (Bogart), the owner, hears the song, rushes over to Sam and loudly reminds him that he was never to play that song again.

MEMORABLE LINES—Ilsa's husband talks privately with Rick:

Victor (Henreid): . . . It is perhaps a strange circumstance that we should be in love with the same woman. The first evening I came to this cafe, I knew there was something between you and Ilsa. I ask only one thing. I want my wife to be safe. I ask you, as a favor, to use the letters to take her away from Casablanca.
Rick: You love her that much?
Victor: Yes, I love her that much.

TAKE NOTE—The budget for this movie was so small they couldn't use a real plane in the background at the airport. A small cardboard cutout gives the illusion that it is real and midgets served as crew preparing plane for the take-off.

TRIVIA QUIZ—All actors in this movie are now dead, but one who was considered for Rick's role is still living at age 89. Who is he? (Answer No. 14)

> *Character may be manifested in the great moments, but is made in the small ones.* —WILLIAM PENN

26

Citizen Kane

Drama 1941

Director: Orson Welles

Starring: Orson Welles, Joseph Cotten, Ruth Warwick,
Dorothy Comingore, Everett Sloan, Ray Collins,
Agnes Moorehead, George Coulouris

● ●

STORY CONCEPT—A young man takes control of the world's sixth-largest private fortune. He builds a newspaper empire, marries the niece of the U.S. president, and runs for governor of the state of New York. He's defeated in the race because his infidelities to his wife are revealed to the public.

THEME—Those who seek power as an end are not always capable of being faithful in love.

FAVORITE SCENE—Political boss, James W. Gettys (Collins), finds out about Charles Kane's (Welles) affair with Susan Alexander (Comingore) and brings Kane's wife, Emily (Warrick), to the apartment to confront him. In spite of threats of exposure, Kane refuses to withdraw from the governor's race.

MEMORABLE LINES—Guardian Walter Thatcher (Coulouris) makes editor Charles Kane aware of his financial losses. Kane replies, "You're right, I did lose a million dollars last year. I expect to lose a million dollars this year. You know, Mr. Thatcher, at the rate of a million dollars a year, I'll have to close this place in sixty years."

TAKE NOTE—Orson Welles, who produced, directed, and co-wrote the screenplay, had never appeared in a movie before. Neither had six of the other leading players listed above.

TRIVIA QUIZ—What is the last word that the forlorn Kane uttered twice just before dying? (Answer No. 15)

We had a lot in common. I loved him and he loved him.

—SHELLY WINTERS

The Country Girl

Drama 1954

Director: George Seaton

Starring: Grace Kelly, Bing Crosby, William Holden

• •

STORY CONCEPT—A director is convinced that the only actor who can bring his play to life is an alcoholic with a poor image of himself. Reluctantly, he seeks the help of the man's wife whom he has fallen in love with. Together they get him on the road to acting in the hopes that he'll recover.

THEME—A person with an addiction often blames the past because of his or her inability to cope with the present.

FAVORITE SCENE—Director Bernie Dodd (Holden) learns that Frank Elgin (Crosby) has been lying to him about his wife, Georgie (Kelly), and his addiction to alcohol. Bernie offers his apologies to Georgie for berating her and blaming her for Frank's failures.

MEMORABLE LINES—Bernie meets his match, Georgie, for the first time.

Bernie: You try to look like an old lady and you're not. You shouldn't wear your hair like that. There are two kinds of women—those who pay too much attention to themselves, and those who don't pay enough.
Georgie: Say, that's quite a pearl of wisdom. May I quote you?

TAKE NOTE—Grace Kelly, known for her incredible beauty, informed MGM that if they didn't loan her to Paramount for the role of Georgie she would quit the movies. They allowed her to play the role and she won the Best Actress Award for her performance.

TRIVIA QUIZ—Who did Bing Crosby lose the Oscar to that year, and for what film? (Answer No. 16)

I owe my success to this: I never gave or took an excuse.

—FLORENCE NIGHTINGALE

The Dark Mirror
Thriller 1946

Director: Robert Siodmak

Starring: Olivia de Havilland, Lew Ayres, Thomas Mitchell, Charles Evans

● ●

STORY CONCEPT—A prominent physician is murdered, and eyewitnesses identify a female suspect who has an identical twin. Neither of the twins will confess to the killing.

THEME—Who you are and who others think you are is not always the same.

FAVORITE SCENE—Lt. Stevenson (Mitchell) confronts Ruth (de Havilland) with the murder of Dr. Peralta and learns that she has an alibi. He is shocked when he meets her identical twin.

MEMORABLE LINES—Lt. Stevenson tries to get Dr. Elliott (Ayres), the psychologist, involved in the murder case.

Stevenson: What about the one you like?
Elliott: What about it?
Stevenson: Suppose she's innocent.
Elliott: There's no particular reason to believe she's in danger.
Stevenson: Living with a killer? If one of them killed with a knife, don't you think there's a chance she would kill again, even her sister if she got nervous about it? (His statement strikes a nerve with Dr. Elliott and he agrees to help.)

TAKE NOTE—Olivia de Havilland, who plays both the guilty and the innocent twin, won Best Actress for another film produced that year, *To Each His Own*.

TRIVIA QUIZ—Who went backstage at the Academy Awards to congratulate de Havilland on her performance and was snubbed by her? (Answer No. 17)

> *She lacks confidence, she craves admiration insatiably. She lives on the reflection of herself in the eyes of others. She does not dare to be herself.* —ANAIS NIN

Dark Passage

Thriller/Romance 1947

Director: Delmer Daves

Starring: Humphrey Bogart, Lauren Bacall, Bruce Bennett, Agnes Moorehead, Tom D'Andrea

● ●

STORY CONCEPT—While escaping from San Quentin, a wrongly convicted wife killer receives unexpected help from a landscape artist. The escapee undergoes plastic surgery to hide his identity until he can find his wife's real killer.

THEME—Persons, unjustly condemned, take risks to prove their innocence.

FAVORITE SCENE—Sam (D'Andrea), a talkative taxi driver, believes in Vincent Parry's (Bogart) innocence and leads him to a mysterious and frightening Dr. Walter Coley. The doctor has been barred from the medical profession, but for $200 he alters Parry's looks.

MEMORABLE LINES—Irene Jansen (Bacall), Parry's lovely benefactor, reacts to his new identity.

Irene (staring at his face): It's unbelievable!
Parry: Don't get any ideas. I like yours just the way it is.

TAKE NOTE—Bogart's full face is not seen until 62 minutes into the film.

TRIVIA QUIZ—Why does Irene Jansen harbor a convicted criminal? (Answer No. 18)

> *There is no greater loan than a sympathetic ear.*
>
> —FRANK TYGER

The Day the Earth Stood Still

Science Fiction 1951

Director: Robert Wise

Starring: Michael Rennie, Patricia Neal, Hugh Marlow, Sam Jaffe, Billy Gray

● ●

STORY CONCEPT—A spaceship lands in Washington, D.C., carrying a representative who warns earthlings of pending destruction if they don't stop aggression.

THEME—Restraints on man's power are necessary to his survival.

FAVORITE SCENE—Young Billy (Gray) takes the new boarder, Mr. Carpenter-Klaatu (Rennie), to Arlington Cemetery where Billy's father is buried. At Lincoln's Memorial, Mr. Carpenter reads the words and says he would like to meet that man, Lincoln.

MEMORABLE LINES—At the boarding house, as the landlady shows Mr. Carpenter his room.

Landlady: You're a long way from home.
Mr. Carpenter-Klaatu: How do you know?
Landlady: I can recognize a New England accent a mile away. (Klaatu smiles.)

TAKE NOTE—Twentieth Century Fox producer Julian Blaustein chose to make this movie based on a story in *Astounding Magazine* by Harry Bates because it was set on Earth and therefore relatively inexpensive to make. Bates was paid $500 for the rights.

TRIVIA QUIZ—Why do some viewers of this film feel that Klaatu is a Christ figure? (Answer No. 19)

We have grasped the mystery of the atom and rejected the Sermon on the Mount. —GENERAL OMAR N. BRADLEY

The Desperate Hours

Drama 1955

Director: William Wyler

Starring: Humphrey Bogart, Fredric March, Martha Scott, Arthur Kennedy, Mary Murphy, Gig Young, Dewey Martin, Robert Middleton

● ●

STORY CONCEPT—Three escaped convicts invade a private home and hold the occupants hostage. They underestimate the courage of the hostages, especially the father who stands up to them.

THEME—The choice to do right has a price, but it's never wrong.

FAVORITE SCENE—Dan Hilliard (March) gets the money that Griffin (Bogart) needs to make a getaway and tricks one of the other convicts to go outside. After doing so, he confronts Griffin, who is holding his son, with a gun that's not actually loaded.

MEMORABLE LINES—Hilliard threatens Griffin near the end of the film.

Hilliard: I never understood how your mind worked till now. I want to kill you. If anything happens to my family, I'll kill you, so help me God!
Griffin: I gotcha. We understand, all the way. (Hilliard leaves.)
Griffin (to Mrs. Hilliard [Scott]): Lady, you didn't know what a tough bird you married.
Mrs. Hilliard: No, I didn't.

TAKE NOTE—Fredric March began his 50-year acting career after suffering from an acute appendicitis attack. He was a bank teller at the time. To distract his attention from the operation, he visualized himself as a great actor. It worked!

TRIVIA QUIZ—What was March's big break that caused him to switch from the stage to movies? (Answer No. 20)

Courage is the virtue which champions the cause of right.

—CICERO

The Diary of Anne Frank

Biography/Drama 1959

Director: George Stevens

Starring: Millie Perkins, Shelly Winters, Joseph Schildraut, Diane Baker, Richard Beymer, Lou Jacobi, Ed Wynn

• •

STORY CONCEPT—In Amsterdam, during the Second World War, the Frank family hides from the Germans for two years in an attic over a factory without being discovered. Two other families join them, and Anne, thirteen years old, records the day-by-day activities in her diary.

THEME—Close relationships formed under difficult circumstances reveal and sometimes develop character.

FAVORITE SCENE—Anne (Perkins) and her family celebrate Hanukkah, their Jewish holiday. According to the custom, Anne gives each of the seven a present from her meager possessions.

MEMORABLE LINES—Anne to Peter Van Daan (Beymer): "When I can't stand another moment of being cooped up I just think myself outside. The wonderful thing is, you can have it any way you want it. I took it for granted—the flowers, the trees."

TAKE NOTE—All of the attic scenes of this movie were shot in the same attic that the real Anne Frank and the others stayed in during the war.

TRIVIA QUIZ—While hidden in the attic, what two gifts brought by their hosts fascinated the Frank family and the others? (Answer No. 21)

Sharing what you have is more important than what you have.
—ALBERT M. WELLS, JR.

Only those who will risk going too far can possibly find out how far one can go.
—T. S. ELIOT

East of Eden

Drama 1955

Director: Elia Kazan

Starring: James Dean, Raymond Massey, Julie Harris,
Richard Davalos, Jo Van Fleet

• •

STORY CONCEPT—Twin brothers compete for their father's acceptance and a girl's love. The father favors one of his sons, but ironically the growing process proves fatal to the adored brother and the misunderstood brother heals.

THEME—Acceptance that is dependent on one's idea of what's right is straining on relationships.

FAVORITE SCENE—Cal Trask (Dean) follows a woman to a brothel where he is thrown out because he's too young. He sneaks back in and finds the "madam" of the establishment. She turns out to be his mother, whom he never knew.

MEMORABLE LINES—After Cal stays out all night, his father, Adam (Massey), makes him read the Bible with reference to confession of sins. Cal defies him.

Father: You're bad!
Cal: You're right. I am bad. I knew that for a long time.
Father: I didn't mean that. I spoke in anger.
Cal: It's true. Aaron is the good one.

TAKE NOTE—*East of Eden* was James Dean's first starring role.

TRIVIA QUIZ—What Bible story is John Steinbeck's *East of Eden* based upon? (Answer No. 22)

> *To expect life to be tailored to our specifications is to invite frustration.* —ANONYMOUS

Edge of Darkness
War 1943

Director: Lewis Milestone

Starring: Ann Sheridan, Errol Flynn, Walter Huston, Helmut Dantine, Judith Anderson

● ●

STORY CONCEPT—A small fishing village in Norway is occupied by the Germans during World War II. A number of planned executions of the town's citizens causes the townspeople to fight for their freedom and overcome.

THEME—People united in a fight for right can conquer.

FAVORITE SCENE—A retired schoolteacher resists the Nazis. He's beaten and all of his belongings are burned in the city square. The local pastor, who walks past the armed guards and takes his broken body to a safe haven, halts his execution.

MEMORABLE LINES—Karen Stansgard (Sheridan) is late for a meeting at the farmhouse. When she arrives, her fiancé, Gunnar Brugge (Flynn), learns that a German soldier has raped her.

Gunnar (enraged): I know the man! I know him! (He rushes to the gun box.)
Karen (calming him down): Now is not the time for revenge. You said yourself, in these times we must be like steel, like steel. Were they just words, Gunnar?

TAKE NOTE—Errol Flynn, who starred in five war movies, failed his physical when he attempted to join the military during World War II. A book was written accusing him of being a Nazi agent and collaborator. David Niven, a fellow actor, answered this charge by stating that most actors wouldn't be capable as guides to the bathroom, much less being spies.

TRIVIA QUIZ—Whose voice is heard on the radio encouraging the Norwegians not to give up? (Answer No. 23)

> *Success is never found. Failure is never fatal. Courage is the only thing.* —SIR WINSTON CHURCHILL

35

A Face in the Crowd

Drama 1957

Director: Elia Kazan

Starring: Andy Griffith, Patricia Neal, Anthony Franciosa, Walter Matthau, Lee Remick

• •

STORY CONCEPT—A small-town radio producer decides to take her interview program to a local jail where she meets Larry "Lonesome" Rhodes, a fast-drinking, big-mouthed drifter and hustler. She primes him for his own radio program, then takes him to the big-time in Memphis for his own highly-rated TV show. Realizing he has a power to persuade, he runs roughshod over all that get in his way, including the promoter who got him there.

THEME—Power without self-control leads to destruction.

FAVORITE SCENE—During an advertising meeting, "Lonesome" (Griffith) grabs one of the sponsor's vitamin pills, swallows it, and begins acting like a high-powered sex machine. His approach convinces the ad agency to change their strategy to a more highly charged campaign.

MEMORABLE LINES—"Lonesome" Rhodes explains to his promoter, Marsha (Neal), why he didn't marry her.

Rhodes: I was afraid to marry you. That's the truth, the dirt road, cotton-picking truth. You're so critical of me.
Marsha: The last time you said you were afraid not to . . . You're getting to be all the things you harpooned.
Rhodes: You see what I mean. The bigger I get, the smaller you make me feel.

TAKE NOTE—In this movie, both Andy Griffith and Lee Remick made their film debuts.

TRIVIA QUIZ—What is the sign on the wall of Rhodes' penthouse? (Answer No. 24)

> *The secret of success is sincerity. Once you can fake that, you've got it made.* —JEAN GIRAUDOUX

The Farmer's Daughter

Comedy/Romance 1947

Director: H. C. Potter

Starring: Loretta Young, Joseph Cotten, Charles Bickford,
Ethel Barrymore, Harry Shannon

● ●

STORY CONCEPT—A young Swedish girl gets a job as the housekeeper for a wealthy congressman and begins taking an interest in politics, which eventually leads her to run for office against her employer who has fallen in love with her.

THEME—All is fair in love and politics.

FAVORITE SCENE—Katrin Holstrom (Young) gives Congressman Glen Morley (Cotten) a massage after he falls through the ice while watching her skate. Joseph Clancey (Bickford), Morley's valet, observes with delight.

MEMORABLE LINES—Katrin quits her campaign for Congress and retreats to her father's farm after being slandered by the press. Glen follows her and talks to Mr. Holstrom (Shannon).

Mr. Holstrom: Then you want her to quit, too.
Glen: I thought it would be the easiest thing for Katie.
Mr. Holstrom: The easiest thing! The easiest thing when I came here is to let the earth lie dead and unplowed and not to have a family.
Katrin: Are you trying to make me feel ashamed?
Mr. Holstrom: Ya, ashamed for quitting! If you want to be in Congress, you fight. If you don't want to fight for the truth you shouldn't be in Congress!

TAKE NOTE—Loretta Young began acting at age 13, and played in 97 movies before launching a successful career in television.

TRIVIA QUIZ—What advice does Glen give to Katrin on speaking in public? (Answer No. 25)

If you want the rainbow, you gotta put up with the rain.

—DOLLY PARTON

Fear Strikes Out

Biography/Drama/Sports 1957

Director: Robert Mulligan

Starring: Anthony Perkins, Karl Malden, Norma Moore,
Perry Wilson, Adam Williams

● ●

STORY CONCEPT—A father's unfulfilled dream to become a major league ball player leads him to be hypercritical of his son who reaches the majors in spite of never satisfying his father. The son has a nervous breakdown, but recovers and plays again when he realizes the primary cause of his problem is his father.

THEME—The attempt to meet the standards of others can cause one to lose one's own identity.

FAVORITE SCENE—During a therapy session, Jimmy (Perkins) and Doctor Brown (Williams) explore Jimmy's relationship with his father (Malden). Jimmy resists blaming his father for being so hard on him and flees the office, but once he realizes the irony of the relationship he returns and begins the road to recovery.

MEMORABLE LINES—Jimmy explains to Mary (Moore) why they can't marry:

Jimmy: We would have to live in hotels, travel, and the competition is terrific!
Mary: You're terrific!
Jimmy: We'd have to live with my folks, four people living in the same house. Impossible! (Pause) Let's get married now!

TAKE NOTE—When young Jimmy Piersall was in little league, he taunted pitchers so badly that he wore a protective helmet because he feared being hit by a ball thrown by the pitcher. Twenty years later, the helmet became standard equipment.

TRIVIA QUIZ—What major league ball team did Jimmy Piersall spend most of his 17-year career with? (Answer No. 26)

The last of our human freedoms is to choose our attitude in any given circumstances. —VICTOR FRANKL

The Fighting Sullivans

Drama/War 1944

Director: Lloyd Bacon

Starring: Thomas Mitchell, Anne Baxter, Selena Royale,
Edward Ryan, Ward Bond

• •

STORY CONCEPT—The true story of five brothers who grow up in the small town of Waterloo, Iowa. When America enters the Second World War, all of them enlist in the navy. They get permission to serve on the same ship, which later sinks with all five aboard.

THEME—Strong family ties and a devotion to country promote the supreme sacrifice.

FAVORITE SCENE—Al (Ryan), the youngest of the five brothers, invites his new girlfriend, Katherine Mary (Baxter), to a family dinner. His brothers tease him unmercifully. Katherine Mary takes it seriously and runs out crying. Al runs after her.

MEMORABLE LINES—A Navy Lieutenant (Bond) brings a telegram to the Sullivan home.

Lieutenant: Bad news
Mother (Royale): Which one?
Lieutenant: All of them.
Father (Mitchell, after a long pause): I have been the conductor on the Illinois Central for thirty-three years and haven't missed a day in all that time. Excuse me.

TAKE NOTE—After the death of the five brothers, a new ship, *The Sullivans*, was launched in their memory. It never experienced severe damage.

TRIVIA QUIZ—What rule did the navy institute after the five Sullivan brothers were killed on the same ship? (Answer No. 27)

> *Greater love has no man than this, that he lay down his life for his friends.* —JESUS

Follow the Sun

Sports/Biography 1951

Director: Sidney Landfield

Starring: Glenn Ford, Anne Baxter, Dennis O'Keefe,
June Havoc, Larry Keating

● ●

STORY CONCEPT—Ben Hogan (Ford), a shy golfer, wins his first major golf tournament at age thirty-five. He survives a head-on collision with a bus and wins the U.S. open for the fourth time. Based on a true story.

THEME—One comes to value people more through personal tragedy.

FAVORITE SCENE—Sports columnist Jay Dexter (Keating) takes digs at Hogan, calling him the "Texas Iceburg" and "Mechanical Man." In spite of this, Hogan and his wife, Valerie (Baxter), try to be friendly toward him and he accuses Hogan of buttering him up. Angered, Hogan walks away but Valerie, his number one supporter, gives Dexter a well-deserved chewing out.

MEMORABLE LINES—In the hospital after his accident, Hogan is touched to receive flowers from people he's never met. He says to his wife, "I should have taken my eye off the ball and taken a good look at people. It took a ten-ton bus to wake me up to this. Those people (pause), I'd like to play again—just for them."

TAKE NOTE—The real golfer, Hogan, was a consultant on the film and practiced with Ford twice a day to teach him his mannerisms. Hogan had 61 victories and won 9 major titles.

TRIVIA QUIZ—What is the significance of the movie's title, *Follow the Sun?* (Answer No. 28)

The breakfast of champions is not cereal, it's obstacles.

—JOHN MASON

For Whom the Bell Tolls
Romance/War 1943

Director: Sam Wood

Starring: Gary Cooper, Ingrid Bergman, Katina Paxinou,
Akim Tamiroff

● ●

STORY CONCEPT—An American professor, who is also a dynamite expert, fights for democracy in the Spanish Civil War and meets a young Spanish refugee. Amongst their involvement in the guerilla fighting, they fall deeply in love.

THEME—Love may enter one's life in the most unlikely of places.

FAVORITE SCENE—Maria (Bergman) tearfully relates to Robert Jordan (Cooper) how she was raped and her father murdered. Her short hair is the badge of her shame. Robert tells her he loves her short hair while stroking it gently.

MEMORABLE LINES—Pilar (Paxinou), the backbone of the resistance movement, tells Maria about the evolution of love. "Things tire me. One of them is to be old and ugly. I was born ugly. Do you know how an ugly woman feels? He thinks you're beautiful, and one day he sees you as ugly as you really are. Then you see yourself as ugly as he sees you and you lose your man and your feeling."

TAKE NOTE—Ernest Hemingway, author of the book, *For Whom the Bell Tolls*, handpicked Cooper and Bergman for the film. Paxinou won the Best Supporting Actress award, a well-deserved honor.

TRIVIA QUIZ—Where was *For Whom the Bell Tolls* filmed? (Answer No. 29)

> *This—this was what made life: a moment of quiet, the water falling in the fountain, the girl's voice—a moment of captured beauty. He who is truly wise will never let such moments to escape.*
> —LOUIS L'AMOUR

Friendly Persuasion

Drama/Comedy 1956

Director: William Wyler

Starring: Gary Cooper, Dorothy McGuire, Anthony Perkins, Phyllis Love, Richard Eyer, Mark Richman, Robert Middleton

●●●●●●●●●●●●●●●●●●●●■●■●●●●●●●●●●●●●●●●●●●●

STORY CONCEPT—A Quaker family in southern Indiana faces a challenge to their faith when music, horseracing, gambling, and the Civil War come knocking at their door.

THEME—The conflict between religious beliefs and tradition is tested when emotional temptations come into play.

FAVORITE SCENE—The elders of the church visit the Birdwell family and hear an organ being played in the attic. Jesse Birdwell (Cooper) begins to pray loudly hoping to drown out the sound. One of the elders compliments his prayer, saying that it lifted him so close to heaven he could hear the harps.

MEMORABLE LINES—Birdwell's daughter, Mattie (Love), and the neighbor's son, Gard (Richman), cease playing the organ in the attic while Jesse and Eliza (McGuire) sit quietly below.

Eliza: What are they doing?
Jesse (expressionless) Silent prayer? (Eliza glares at Jesse, rejecting that idea.)

TAKE NOTE—Gary Cooper made 83 movies before this one, in which he was apprehensive about portraying a father for the first time.

TRIVIA QUIZ –Which pop singer of the fifties sings the theme song for the movie? (Answer No. 30)

> *Following the path of least resistance is what makes men and rivers crooked.* —LARRY BIELAT

Gaslight

Thriller 1944

Director: George Cukor

Starring: Ingrid Bergman, Charles Boyer, Joseph Cotten, Angela Lansbury, Dame May Whitty

● ●

STORY CONCEPT—An attractive heiress finds that her suitor is interested not only in her charm, but also in a house she's inherited from her murdered aunt. Her aunt was murdered ten years before and jewels were stolen which were never recovered. She marries her suitor and his plan to drive her to insanity fails when she meets Brian Cameron (Cotten), a Scotland Yard detective, who helps her solve the mystery.

THEME—A doubtful mind, unduly influenced, leads to insecurity and possible psychological illness.

FAVORITE SCENE—Gregory Anton (Boyer) accuses his wife, Paula (Bergman), of hiding a picture on the mantle, which he has blamed her of doing twice before. He summons the cook and the maid who swear on the Bible that they did not take the picture. The psychological effects of his accusations are detrimental to his wife.

MEMORABLE LINES—Gregory continues his assault on Paula's sanity by treating her like a sick person.

Paula: Are you trying to tell me I'm insane?
Gregory: I'm trying hard not to tell you that (pause) your mother died in an asylum.

TAKE NOTE—Lansbury, in her debut as the maid, was nominated for Best Supporting Actress. She was 17 and had never acted before. For many years, she starred in her own TV series, "Murder She Wrote."

TRIVIA QUIZ—What frightens Paula each night when she is alone? (Answer No. 31)

Fear is the most damnable, damaging thing to human personality in the whole world. —WILLIAM FAULKNER

Gentleman's Agreement
Drama/Romance 1947

Director: Elia Kazan

Starring: Gregory Peck, Dorothy McGuire, John Garfield, Celeste Holm, Albert Dekker, June Havoc, Harold Vermilyea

● ●

STORY CONCEPT—A widowed journalist, assigned to produce a series of articles on anti-Semitism, assumes the identity of a Jew for six weeks.

THEME—A hidden agenda of bigotry is more difficult to combat than blatant narrow-mindedness.

FAVORITE SCENE—Dave Goldman (Garfield), a Jew, asks Kathy (McGuire) what she does when she becomes outraged at someone who tells a racist joke. "Nothing," she replies emptily.

MEMORABLE LINES—Journalist Phil Green (Peck) lunches with Anne Dettrey (Holm), a fashion editor. Lou Jordan (Vermilyea) joins them.

Lou: (to Phil): You were in public relations, weren't you?
Phil: What makes you say that?
Lou: I don't know. You seem like a clever sort of guy.
Phil: What makes you think I wasn't a G.I.?
Lou: Don't get me wrong. Some of my best friends are . . .
Anne (interrupts): Some of your best friends are Methodist, but you wouldn't bother to say it!

TAKE NOTE—Several Jewish studio heads asked Producer Darryl Zanuck to give up making the film for fear it would stir up a hornet's nest. The movie was made and went on to win Best Picture.

TRIVIA QUIZ—Where does the title of the film come from? (Answer No. 32)

> *I cannot do everything, but still I can do something; and because I cannot do everything, I will not refuse to do the something that I can do.* —EDWARD EVERETT HALE

Giant

Drama 1956

Director: George Stevens

Starring: Elizabeth Taylor, Rock Hudson, James Dean, Mercedes McCambridge, Chill Wills, Dennis Hopper

●●●●●●●●●●●●●●●●●●●●●●●●●●●●●●●●

STORY CONCEPT—In Texas, over a span of 25 years, a cattle baron and a high society gal from Maryland face conflict with Texans and Mexicans, rich neighbors and poor, and with each other, but they survive to grow older and wiser.

THEME—Tradition passes slowly, but the sands of time and truth wear it down.

FAVORITE SCENE—Cattle baron Bick Benedict (Hudson) goes to the home of a Maryland surgeon to purchase a prize stallion. He meets the lovely daughter, Leslie (Taylor), and the sparks begin to fly in more ways than one. Breakfast comes to a halt when a debate arises about how Texas landowners obtain their wealth.

MEMORABLE LINES—Leslie, the outsider, is rejected when she attempts to challenge the taboos of the west and joins in on the private conversation of men.

Leslie (muttering loudly): This cavemen stuff dates back 100,000 years!
Bick: You're not well! You're tired!
Leslie: That's right, ladies dismissed. Send the children up to bed so the grownups can talk!

TAKE NOTE—James Dean, who plays Jett Rink, was killed in a fiery auto accident two weeks after the film was completed.

TRIVIA QUIZ—What does Jett discover on the small piece of land that the deceased Luz Benedict (McCambridge) gave to him. (Answer No. 33)

Everything changes but change itself. —JOHN F. KENNEDY

The Glenn Miller Story
Romance/Musical/Biography 1954

Director: Anthony Mann

Starring: James Stewart, June Allyson, Harry Morgan, Charles Drake, Barton MacLane

● ●

STORY CONCEPT—True story of songwriter and musician, Glenn Miller, who had his ups and downs in his work life until the late '30s when the Glenn Miller Band became famous.

THEME—A committed focus on a dream, which you have the ability to achieve, makes it come true.

FAVORITE SCENE—Glenn Miller's (Stewart) military band plays the St. Louis Blues for troops on review before General Arnold (MacLane). The general likes it so much that he assigns Miller to entertain troops overseas, despite objections by Miller's commanding officer.

MEMORABLE LINES—In the hospital, after Helen Miller (Allyson) loses her baby and learns she can't have any more:

Glenn: I want two kids, a boy and a girl.
Helen (tearfully): I can't have children!
Glenn: There'll be two kids meant for us somewhere in the world and we'll find them.

TAKE NOTE—Several entertainers play themselves in this film: Louis Armstrong, Frances Langford, Gene Krupa, and Ben Pollock.

TRIVIA QUIZ—What is wrong with Miller's army band playing while Negro and Caucasian soldiers march side by side? (Answer No. 34)

> *I wake up every morning and know where I'm going and I'm not at the mercy of someone else.* —MERRITT WIESE

Going My Way
Drama/Musical 1944

Director: Leo McCarey

Starring: Bing Crosby, Barry Fitzgerald, Risë Stevens, Frank McHugh

● ●

STORY CONCEPT—A young Irish-American priest is sent to a parish to replace an old Irish-born priest. Their conflicting personalities create problems and the older priest asks for a replacement.

THEME—Youth and enthusiasm present a challenge to the tradition-bound older person.

FAVORITE SCENE—Father Fitzgibbon (Fitzgerald) runs away when he discovers that after 45 years of service he is being replaced. A policeman finds him and brings him back, where Father O'Malley (Crosby) convinces him that he is loved and needed.

MEMORABLE LINES—Father Fitzgibbon talks facetiously about the puppies a widow has given to him and Father O'Malley: "The joy of giving is indeed a pleasure, especially when you're giving something you don't want anyway."

TAKE NOTE—This film swept the Oscars in 1945, getting Best Picture, Best Director, Best Actor (Crosby), Best Supporting Actor (Fitzgerald), and Best Song ("Swing On a Star").

TRIVIA QUIZ—What is the title of the sequel to this film starring Crosby and Ingrid Bergman? (Answer No. 35)

Nobody knows the age of the human race, but all agree that it is old enough to know better. —ANONYMOUS

The Grapes of Wrath
Drama 1940

Director: John Ford

Starring: Henry Fonda, Jane Darwell, Russell Simpson, John Carradine

• •

STORY CONCEPT—During the Great Depression, an Oklahoma family loses their farm and moves to California to find jobs. Their challenging journey encompasses rejection, dire poverty, death, and little opportunity for work, but they persevere.

THEME—Poverty and ignorance are ripe fruits for unjustness.

FAVORITE SCENE—Pa Joad (Simpson) buys a fifteen-cent loaf of bread for a dime from a sympathetic waitress. His grandchildren eye the candy on the shelf and she sells him two pieces for a penny. A truck driver nearby knows that the candy is a nickel each and says so. The waitress tells him to mind his own business. The driver gives her a big tip as he leaves.

MEMORABLE LINES—Tom Joad (Fonda) and his family run away from a transient camp that is about to be burned by locals.

Tom: Ma, There comes a time when a man gets mad.
Ma (Darwell): But Tom, you told me, you promised.
Tom: I know. If there was a law they was workin' with maybe we could take it, but it ain't the law. They're workin' away our spirits, tryin' to make us cringe and crawl, takin' away our decency.

TAKE NOTE—The scene in the movie where Tommy and his Ma see each other for the last time is so moving that the script girl cried and director Ford walked away. Fonda speculated that he was also crying.

TRIVIA QUIZ—What does Ma Joad do just before leaving for California? (Answer No. 36)

> *Hold on with a bulldog grip, and chew and choke as much as possible.* —ABRAHAM LINCOLN

Heaven Knows, Mr. Allison

Drama/War 1957

Director: John Huston

Starring: Robert Mitchum, Deborah Kerr

• •

STORY CONCEPT—A marine from a sunken submarine washes ashore on a deserted island and finds a Catholic nun who has been left behind. The Japanese invade and establish the island as their weather station. The marine sabotages the enemy's heavy weapons, and he and the nun stay hidden in a cave until help arrives.

THEME—People from two different backgrounds and in danger share a commitment for survival.

FAVORITE SCENE—Sister Angela (Kerr) and Allison (Mitchum) talk about their close relationship. He asks her not to take her final vows, but to marry him instead. She says no and shows him her ring, indicating that she is married to Christ, her first love.

MEMORABLE LINES—Mr. Allison and Sister Angela talk about their pasts.

Allison: I was left on Allison Street. Illegitimate, but I was born. Had no parents. But I had a D.I. [drill instructor] who said I would hate him. He was right. But he was right!
Sister Angela: I had a D.I.—Mother Superior. We called her the holy terror. (Allison looks amused. He didn't know that nuns could joke around.)

TAKE NOTE—The movie was filmed in Tabago, British West Indies. A giant turtle lassoed by Mitchum dragged him through brush and nettle for a quarter of a mile, badly cutting him.

TRIVIA QUIZ—What are the last words that Sister Angela says to the wounded Mr. Allison as the rescue is completed? (Answer No. 37)

The fragrance of what you give away stays with you.

—EARL ALLEN

Hondo

Western/Romance 1953

Director: John Farrow

Starring: John Wayne, Geraldine Page, Ward Bond,
Michael Pate, Lee Aaker

● ●

STORY CONCEPT—A half-Apache army scout risks his life against Apaches to help an endangered woman and her son in the wilderness. The Indians think he's the woman's husband and father to the child, and the chief is so impressed with the son's bravery that he spares the lives of the adults.

THEME—The difference between life and death is sometimes a small thread.

FAVORITE SCENE—Hondo (Wayne) throws the six-year-old Johnny Lowe (Aaker) into the water and watches him flounder while Johnny's mother, Angie (Page), screams for Hondo to help. He asks her why she doesn't help and learns that she can't swim either. Hondo stares at her and she runs away quickly, fearing that he might throw her in also.

MEMORABLE LINES—Angie feels sorry for Sam, Hondo's dog, as the dog watches him eat.

Hondo: I'd rather you wouldn't feed him.
Angie: You mean you don't want him to take from strangers?
Hondo: No, I don't feed him myself. He's independent and I want him to stay that way.
Angie: Everyone needs someone.

TAKE NOTE—This movie, based on a story by Louis L'Amour, a popular Western writer, was filmed in Camargo, Mexico.

TRIVIA QUIZ—Who is Hondo's dog? (Answer No. 38)

> *Men strive for peace, but it is their enemies that give them strength, and I think if man no longer had enemies, he would have to invent them, for his strength only grows from struggle.*

> —LOUIS L'AMOUR

The Human Comedy

Drama 1943

Director: Clarence Brown

Starring: Mickey Rooney, Fay Bainter, Van Johnson, Frank Morgan, James Craig, Donna Reed, Jackie "Butch" Jenkins

• •

STORY CONCEPT—A small-town high school boy, whose older brother has gone to war, takes a job as a night messenger for the local telegraph office in order to make ends meet financially. The hardest part of his job—delivering telegrams to the families who have lost loved ones in the war—makes him grow up fast.

THEME—Wartime quickly changes youths into adults.

FAVORITE SCENE—Homer McCauley (Rooney) delivers a telegram to an uneducated Mexican woman. She asks Homer to read the message for her, telling her of the death of her son who was killed in action.

MEMORABLE LINES—Katie McCauley (Bainter) answers questions from her young son, Ulysses (Jenkins), at bedtime.

Ulysses: Why does Homer have to work?
Katie: Because your father's gone, your brother's in the service, and we need the money to buy food and to help the poor.
Ulysses: Where has my father gone?
Katie: Where we all must go.
Ulysses: If we wait, will he come home?
Katie: Not like you mean, but nothing can take him from us; he lives in our hearts.

TAKE NOTE—Mickey Rooney began acting when he was 15 months old and is still acting today at 80.

TRIVIA QUIZ—What song is sung on the train, which is taking soldiers to the front? (Answer No. 39)

Maturity is the ability to live in someone else's world.

—OREN ARNOLD

Imitation of Life

Drama 1959

Director: Douglas Sirk

Starring: Lana Turner, Juanita Moore, Sandra Dee, Susan Kohner, John Gavin, Robert Alda

● ●

STORY CONCEPT—A struggling actress and her daughter swap lodging for services with an unemployed housekeeper and her daughter. Their future looks bright when the actress gets a break. She opts for stardom rather than love and marriage.

THEME—Climbing the ladder of success leaves close relationships behind.

FAVORITE SCENE—African American Juanita Moore (Johnson) tracks down her white daughter, Sara Jane (Kohner), to a nightclub where she's a dancer. She confronts Sara about her shame of being of mixed race, and makes two requests of her. If anything should happen, contact her friend and employer, Lora Meredith (Turner), and, tearfully, she asks for one last hug.

MEMORABLE LINES—Annie Johnson dresses to go out for the night.

Lora: I never knew you had many friends.
Annie: I belong to the Baptist Church—and several lodges.
Lora: I never knew that.
Annie: You never asked me.

TAKE NOTE—This movie is a remake of the 1934 film with Claudette Colbert, which is based on the novel by Fanny Hurst.

TRIVIA QUIZ—Who was the outstanding professional soloist at the funeral service? (Answer No. 40)

Friends are those rare people who ask how we are and then wait to hear the answer. —ED CUNNINGHAM

The Inn of the Sixth Happiness

Biography/Romance 1958

Director: Mark Robson

Starring: Ingrid Bergman, Curt Jürgens, Robert Donat, Michael David

• •

STORY CONCEPT—A self-appointed missionary saves her money and takes the train from England to China where she operates an inn for travelers. When the Japanese invade northern China, she leads 100 children across the mountains to safety.

THEME—An indomitable spirit can accomplish what seems to be impossible.

FAVORITE SCENE—At the Chinese market, Gladys Aylward (Bergman) experiences culture shock. Women chase her when she touches a child on the head. While trying to escape, she's chased out of a men-only establishment. She also witnesses a public execution.

MEMORABLE LINES—Colonel Lin Nan (Jürgens), who has fallen in love with Gladys, speaks with her about her future plans.

Lin: But what if you marry?
Gladys: That won't happen.
Lin: You've said that before. How can you be sure? Have you ever met anyone you love?
Gladys: Nor anyone who loved me. I'm not attractive that way.
Lin: Don't you know you're beautiful?
Gladys: Once in her life every woman should have that said to her. Thank you for being the one who said it to me.

TAKE NOTE—Gladys Aylward, a British-born maid, had little education and was considered too old by her church board, at age 30, to learn Chinese.

TRIVIA QUIZ—What is unusual about the sleeping arrangements in the inn during wintertime? (Answer No. 41)

One can never consent to creep when one feels an impulse to soar.

—HELEN KELLER

I Remember Mama

Drama 1948

Director: George Stevens

Starring: Irene Dunne, Barbara Bel Geddes, Oscar Homolka, Philip Dorn, Cedric Hardwicke, June Hedin

• •

STORY CONCEPT—The oldest daughter of a Norwegian family wants to be a writer, so she writes about her mother, the heart of the family, who strives hard to make ends meet. The family's life intertwines with the lives of a well-read boarder, three aunts, and an eccentric Uncle Chris (Homolka) who lives in the country.

THEME—The wisdom of age guides the unpredictable emotions of youth.

FAVORITE SCENE—The hospital authorities won't let Mama (Dunne) spend the night in the hospital with her daughter, so she poses as a scrubwoman and slips into the room and sings her little one to sleep with a Norwegian lullaby.

MEMORABLE LINES—Young Dagmar's (Hedin) cat is dying and has to be put to sleep. Mama and Papa (Dorn) discuss how to break the news to her.

Mama: We have to tell her the truth. It's not good to let her grow up thinking I can fix everything.
Papa: That's what I thought all the time.

TAKE NOTE—Barbara Bel Geddes, who plays the writer, Katrin, is best known for her role as Ellie Ewing on the popular television series, "Dallas," during the '70s and '80s.

TRIVIA QUIZ—How does Mr. Hyde (Hardwicke), the boarder, pay his rent? (Answer No. 42)

All that I am or hope to be I owe to my angel mother.

—ABRAHAM LINCOLN

It's a Wonderful Life

Fantasy 1946

Director: Frank Capra

Starring: James Stewart, Donna Reed, Lionel Barrymore, Henry Travers, Thomas Mitchell

STORY CONCEPT—A small-town man yearns to see the world, but the financial bankruptcy his father faces gets in the way of his dream. The man considers suicide, but his guardian angel saves him and paints a picture of how Bedford Falls would have turned out without his influence. The man's spirits are lifted and, surprisingly, he's bailed out financially by an unlikely source.

THEME—A man who has friends is indeed wealthy.

FAVORITE SCENE—George Bailey (Stewart) is torn between his love for Mary (Reed) and his desire to travel. While visiting her, he's unable to express his feelings and leaves. When he returns to claim his forgotten hat, Mary is on the phone with a friend and George recognizes how much he likes her.

MEMORABLE LINES—George, who faces bankruptcy and prison, goes to the river to drown himself, but instead saves his guardian angel (Travers) and takes him to dry out in a neighbor's house.

Neighbor (to angel): How did you fall in?
Angel: I didn't fall in. I jumped in to save George.
George: To what? To save me?
Angel: You didn't go through with it.
George: With what?
Angel: Suicide. That's the reason I jumped in. I knew you'd try to save me.

TAKE NOTE—The inspiration for this film came from the few paragraphs of a Christmas card called "The Greatest Gift."

TRIVIA QUIZ—What is the name of George's guardian angel? (Answer No. 43)

When things go wrong don't go with them. —ANONYMOUS

55

The Jackie Robinson Story

Biography/Sports 1950

Director: Alfred E. Green

Starring: Jackie Robinson, Ruby Dee, Louise Beavers, Minor Watson, Joel Fluellen

● ●

STORY CONCEPT—The true story of Jackie Robinson, the first black man to play major league baseball.

THEME—Those who are disadvantaged and pave the way for others will be aptly rewarded.

FAVORITE SCENE—Jackie Robinson, playing himself in this movie, slides into second base and upsets the second baseman who immediately jumps on him. His teammates, led by a pitcher who swore he'd never play on the same team with a black man, rush onto the field to give him support.

MEMORABLE LINES—Branch Rickey (Watson), president of the Brooklyn Dodgers, explains to Jackie his pacifist role as the first black in the majors.

Jackie: Do you want a player who won't fight back?
Rickey: I want a player who has the guts not to fight back. . . . No matter what happens on the ball field, you can't fight back.

TAKE NOTE—Jackie Robinson helped Brooklyn win six pennants and one World Series during his ten seasons with the team, from 1947 to 1956. He was elected to the Baseball Hall of Fame in 1962.

TRIVIA QUIZ—What advice did Jackie's mother (Beavers) give to him about being the first black in major league baseball? (Answer No. 44)

> *I guess more players lick themselves than are licked by an opposing team. The first thing any man has to know is how to handle himself.* —CONNIE MACK

56

Jim Thorpe—All American
Sports/Drama 1950

Director: Michael Curtiz

Starring: Burt Lancaster, Charles Bickford, Phyllis Thaxter, Steve Cochrane

● ●

STORY CONCEPT—The rise and fall of Jim Thorpe, an Indian boy from Oklahoma, who makes it to the Olympics in Stockholm in 1912, is a true-life depiction. The death of his son, his unwillingness to follow rules, his drinking and a divorce all contribute to his downfall. Still, against all odds, he's recognized as one of our greatest sports figures.

THEME—Natural ability and a burning desire cause one to triumph.

FAVORITE SCENE—Athletic director Pop Warner (Bickford) recognizes the talents of Jim (Lancaster) and asks him to consider staying in school rather than returning to the Indian reservation.

MEMORABLE LINES—Jim walks with Margaret Miller (Thaxter), an attractive student on campus.

Jim: There's something I'd like to tell you.
Margaret: What?
Jim: I think I'm in love with you. I can't be sure. I've never been in love before. Thought you ought to know. (Margaret smiles faintly as he walks away.)

TAKE NOTE—It took Warner Bros. 15 years to find someone right for the part of Jim Thorpe. Thirty years after Thorpe's death in 1953, his Olympic medals were reinstated to his heirs. They had been taken away from him during college because he had accepted money for playing baseball during the summer.

TRIVIA QUIZ—Who performs all of the track and football feats in the film? (Answer No. 45)

Never let yesterday use up today. —RICHARD H. NELSON

Johnny Belinda

Drama 1948

Director: Jean Negulesco

Starring: Jane Wyman, Lew Ayres, Charles Bickford,
Agnes Moorehead, Stephen McNally, Jan Sterling

• •

STORY CONCEPT—A young deaf-mute girl is raped by a local man and becomes pregnant. When the baby is born, the villagers decide to take the child away from her and give him to the attacker and his new wife. The deaf-mute girl kills the abuser and is tried for murder. The testimony of his wife sets her free.

THEME—Justice delayed is not justice denied.

FAVORITE SCENE—Dr. Richardson (Ayres) teaches Belinda (Wyman) sign language. Her father, McDonald (Bickford), marvels that she is not so dumb, and her increased self-esteem is evident from that day on.

MEMORABLE LINES—Belinda's father learns that she's pregnant.

McDonald: The shame of it!
Dr. Richardson: Don't think of yourself! There's only one shame—failing the human being who needs you.

TAKE NOTE—Wyman worked with deaf mutes and used earplugs to shut out sound during the filming of her scenes. She received an Oscar for her performance.

TRIVIA QUIZ—Who did Jane Wyman divorce during production of this film? (Answer No. 46)

Of all earthly music that which reaches farthest into heaven is the beating of a truly loving heart. —HENRY WARD BEECHER

Key Largo
Drama 1948

Director: John Huston

Starring: Humphrey Bogart, Lauren Bacall,
Edward G. Robinson, Claire Trevor,
Lionel Barrymore

● ●

STORY CONCEPT—A returning veteran during World War II goes to the Florida Keys to visit the father and the widow of his wartime buddy, George. A deported racketeer is holding the two of them hostage while waiting for another gangster, who wants to purchase some counterfeit money from him, to arrive. The war vet unwittingly gets involved in the whole confusion.

THEME—One person resisting evil can inspire others to follow suit.

FAVORITE SCENE—Ex-army Major Frank McCloud (Bogart) tells Mr. Temple (Barrymore) and his daughter-in-law, Nora (Bacall), about George's bravery in battle.

MEMORABLE LINES—A hurricane rages outside and McCloud sees the fear on the gangster Rocco's (Robinson) face: "You don't like it, do you, Rocco, the storm. Show it your gun, why don't you? If it doesn't stop, shoot it!"

TAKE NOTE—Bogart and Bacall, who were married, appeared together in her first five films.

TRIVIA QUIZ—How does the gangster's girlfriend (Trevor) help McCloud? (Answer No. 47)

An empty barrel makes the loudest noise. —ANONYMOUS

The Keys of the Kingdom

Drama 1944

Director: John M. Stahl

Starring: Gregory Peck, Thomas Mitchell, Vincent Price, Rosa Stradner, Benson Fong

● — ● ● ● ● ● ● ● ● ● ●

STORY CONCEPT—A young Scottish boy reluctantly joins the priesthood and fails at his first two posts before accepting a mission in China where he finally succeeds as a practical nurse. His humility is a model for his fellow European workers and the Chinese people, especially the children.

THEME—Hardships and determination can become stepping-stones to success.

FAVORITE SCENE—The day before Father Francis Chisholm (Peck) leaves for Scotland, he rereads portions of his journal to Mother Maria-Veronica (Stradner), who has grown to love him despite her aristocratic upbringing. Her facial expressions speak volumes when she tells him that she will never forget him.

MEMORABLE LINES—Dr. Willie Tullock (Mitchell), Father Francis' longtime atheist schoolmate, is mortally wounded.

Willie: Go ahead and pray for yourself. For me, you're wasting your time. I still can't believe in God. Are you mad at me?
Francis: Of course not.
Willie: Are you disappointed I won't let you save me?
Francis: Your salvation will be your doing, not mine.
Willie (with his last breath): Francis, I've never loved you so much as I do now because you haven't tried to bully me into heaven.

TAKE NOTE—This was Peck's first major film nominated for an Academy Award.

TRIVIA QUIZ—What best-selling novel by A.J. Cronin was this film based upon? (Answer No. 48)

Whosoever therefore shall humble himself as this little child, the same is greatest in the kingdom of heaven. —JESUS

King Solomon's Mines
Adventure/Romance 1950

Directors: Compton Bennett and Andrew Marton

Starring: Stewart Granger, Deborah Kerr, Richard Carlson

STORY CONCEPT—In 1897 in Africa, a prim Englishwoman hires a guide to search for her missing husband.

THEME—Loneliness and misunderstanding can turn to love and acceptance.

FAVORITE SCENE—Upper class Elizabeth Curtis (Kerr) begins her trek across Africa dressed in proper English attire. Allan Quatermain (Granger), her guide, orders her to remove her corset and get some proper clothing if she wants to survive the journey.

MEMORABLE LINES—Guide Quatermain turns down the invitation of Goode (Carlson) to lead the search, but listens to Goode's sister, Elizabeth.

Elizabeth: There was one argument he neglected to use.
Quatermain: Oh, what's that?
Elizabeth: Money.
Quatermain: Very good argument.
Elizabeth: What is your usual fee?
Quatermain: 200 pounds. Wouldn't' take it for 500.
Elizabeth: Would you for 5,000? (Pause) You're weakening, aren't you?

TAKE NOTE—The film was shot in Africa and the native Watussis were given major roles with respect and dignity. Granger, a British star, spoke excellent Swahili.

TRIVIA QUIZ—The book, *King Solomon's Mines*, spawned a series of popular African adventure books written by an American who had never stepped foot in Africa? What was the author's name? (Answer No. 49)

And the trouble is, if you don't risk anything, you risk even more.

—ERICA JONG

King's Row

Drama/Romance 1941

Director: Sam Wood

Starring: Robert Cummings, Ronald Reagan, Ann Sheridan,
Betty Field, Claude Rains, Charles Coburn

● ●

STORY CONCEPT—In a small town at the turn of the century, two boyhood friends face tragedies that shake their world. The girlfriend of one of them is murdered by her father and the other is injured in a train accident and has his legs amputated.

THEME—Love and friendship are more powerful than tragedy.

FAVORITE SCENE—Randy Monighan (Sheridan) uses her wisdom and reverse psychology to get Drake McHugh (Reagan) to accept the inheritance that Parris Mitchell (Cummings) offers him, which will help hasten his recovery. She gets Drake, who has lost his legs, to focus on the future rather than on his handicap.

MEMORABLE LINES—Parris reasons with his grandmother's lawyer.

Parris: I never wanted to see King's Row again. I'm afraid of meeting ghosts.
Lawyer: I thought chasing ghosts from people's minds was right in your line.
(Parris, a psychologist, ponders this truth.)

TAKE NOTE—This movie, one of 50, was the high point of Ronald Reagan's acting career spanning 27 years.

TRIVIA QUIZ—What are the words in the movie that became the title of Reagan's 1965 autobiography? (Answer No. 50)

What the student calls a tragedy, the master calls a butterfly.
—RICHARD BACH

Kiss of Death

Drama 1947

Director: Henry Hathaway

Starring: Victor Mature, Richard Widmark, Colleen Gray,
Brian Donlevy

● ●

STORY CONCEPT—A convicted prisoner won't reveal the identity of his fellow jewel thieves, then his wife commits suicide and his two young daughters are placed in foster care. He cooperates with the assistant district attorney and is paroled.

THEME—The consequences of one's actions should be thought about well ahead of time.

FAVORITE SCENE—Nick Bianco (Mature) sits at home in the dark. With his gun in hand, he waits for vengeful killer Tommy Udo (Widmark). A car pulls up; a man gets out, comes through the door, and walks into the light. Bianco's about to shoot when he recognizes D'Angelo (Donlevy), who has come to warn him.

MEMORABLE LINES—Assistant District Attorney D'Angelo assures informant Bianco that another criminal will be blamed for informing.

Bianco: Your side of the fence is almost as dirty as mine.
D'Angelo: With one big difference. We hurt bad people and not good.

TAKE NOTE—Richard Widmark, star of stage and screen, attributes his love for the cinema to his grandmother who began taking him to movies at age three, and to the fact that later on in life he worked as a doorman in a local theater.

TRIVIA QUIZ—Who became Bianco's second wife after his release from prison? (Answer No. 51)

The wages of sin is death. . . Thank God I quit before pay day.
—REAMER LOUIS

The Last Angry Man
Drama 1959

Director: Daniel Mann

Starring: Paul Muni, David Wayne, Luther Adler,
Betsy Palmer, Billy Dee Williams, Joby Baker

STORY CONCEPT—A 68-year-old doctor in a poor section of Brooklyn becomes the subject of a primetime documentary. His medical advice is too radical for the producers, but the sponsors admire his independence.

THEME—A concern for others should take precedence over material gains.

FAVORITE SCENE—TV Producer Woody Thrasher (Wayne) offers Dr. Sam Abelman (Muni) a house as a gift for his 45 years in community service. Abelman calls it a bribe and is adamant about not taking something for nothing.

MEMORABLE LINES—The host of the television show compliments Dr. Abelman on his life of service.

Abelman: I'm just a midget. Compared to this man right here . . . (he points to a photograph.)
TV Host: You mean Dr. Brooks Harlow, your professor at Bellevue.
Abelman: There was a giant, a healer. He used to teach you have to know the whole man: problems, anxieties. He pounded into our thick skulls that, not pills, not medicine, are important, but people, that's important . . .

TAKE NOTE—Paul Muni appeared in only 18 films over a 50-year period, yet he was nominated for Best Actor five times, including his role in *The Last Angry Man*.

TRIVIA QUIZ—Why is Dr. Abelman angry? (Answer No. 52)

> *You may not have saved a lot of money in your life, but if you have saved a lot of heartaches for other folks, you are a pretty rich man.*
>
> —SETH PARKER

64

Laura

Thriller 1944

Director: Otto Preminger

Starring: Gene Tierney, Dana Andrews, Clifton Webb, Vincent Price, Judith Anderson

●●●

STORY CONCEPT—An attractive businesswoman, loved by all, is allegedly killed. The detective investigates her murder with the help of a newspaper columnist and critic.

THEME—Love is one of the strongest motivations for human actions.

FAVORITE SCENE—Detective Mark McPherson (Andrews) interrogates the supposedly dead Laura Hunt (Tierney) when she strolls into her apartment after a weekend in the country. Because of his attraction to her, he wants her to be innocent, but she appears to be the main suspect.

MEMORABLE LINES—Columnist Waldo Lydecker (Webb) to Detective McPherson, who is showing unusual interest in a victim that he's never met:

Lydecker: I hear you've put in a bid for her [Laura's] portrait. You'd better watch it, McPherson. You'll end up in a psychiatric ward. I don't believe they've ever had a patient who fell in love with a corpse.

TAKE NOTE—Clifton Webb, who portrays the columnist, has his first screen appearance in 20 years, and stars in his first talking picture.

TRIVIA QUIZ—Where is the murder weapon hidden? (Answer No. 53)

He who lives to benefit himself confers on the world a benefit when he dies. —TERTULLIAN

A Letter to Three Wives
Drama/Romance 1949

Director: Joseph L. Mankiewicz

Starring: Kirk Douglas, Ann Sothern, Linda Darnell, Paul Douglas, Jeanne Crain, Jeffrey Lynn, Connie Gilchrist, Thelma Ritter

● ●

STORY CONCEPT—Three wives receive a letter from a friend as they are about to set out on an all-day excursion with their children. The friend is a beautiful woman who has left town with one of their husbands. During the day, each of the wives reminisces about life with her husband and wonders who the forsaken one is.

THEME—Reflecting on one's relationship needs to be a priority before that relationship ends, not after.

FAVORITE SCENE—Rita Phipps (Sothern), a soap opera writer, invites her boss to dinner, but forgets that it's her husband George's (Kirk Douglas) birthday. Addie Ross, who's got her eye on him, does not forget. She sends George a record for his collection, along with a note that says, "If music be the food of love, play on."

MEMORABLE LINES—Mrs. Finney (Gilchrist) rebukes her gold-digging daughter, Lora May (Darnell), as she storms from the house. Her neighbor, Sadie (Ritter), overhears the emotional outburst.

Mrs. Finney: Can't we have peace in this house even on New Year's Eve?

Sadie: You got it mixed up with Christmas. New Year's Eve is when people go back to killing each other.

TAKE NOTE—Addie Ross, the husband-stealer, is never actually seen in the movie. Her voice is that of Celeste Holm who at 82 plays Hattie Green, the grandmother on the "Promised Land" TV series.

TRIVIA QUIZ—Which of the three wives did not marry for love? (Answer No. 54)

A successful marriage requires falling in love many times, always with the same person. —MIGNON MCLAUGHLIN

Lifeboat

Drama/War 1944

Director: Alfred Hitchcock

Starring: Tallulah Bankhead, William Bendix, Walter Slezak,
John Hodiak, Hume Cronyn, Mary Anderson,
Henry Hull, Heather Angel, Canada Lee

• •

STORY CONCEPT—Eight survivors of a ship torpedoed by a German submarine rescue the surgeon and captain of the sinking U-boat. The conflict becomes unbearable when they discover that the captain has little regard for human life.

THEME—It is never too late to unite opposing forces and overcome evil.

FAVORITE SCENE—Connie (Bankhead) loses her valuables on the lifeboat, and she responds to the rescue in this way: "Twenty minutes. Good heavens! My nails, my hair, my face. I'm a mess!"

MEMORABLE LINES—The German captain defends dumping the wounded sailor, Gus (Bendix), overboard.

Willie (Sleazak): A poor simple dying without food and water. He's better off dead. (The other survivors beat Willie to death.)
Rittenhouse (Hull): When we killed the German we killed our motor.
Joe (Lee): No, we still have a motor. (He looks up at the sky.)
Connie: It's okay to look up and trust in someone. How about helping him out?

TAKE NOTE—They used only one set in the entire film—a lifeboat. Many in the cast caught pneumonia after constant exposure to the cold water.

TRIVIA QUIZ— What is unusual about the musical score in this film? (Answer No. 55)

> *There is no readier way for a man to bring his own worth into question than by endeavoring to detract from the worth of other men.* —JOHN TILLOTSON

The Long Gray Line

Biography/Drama/Romance 1955

Director: John Ford

Starring: Tyrone Power, Maureen O'Hara, Donald Crisp, Betsy Palmer, William Leslie, Robert Francis

● ●

STORY CONCEPT—Upon his arrival in America, an Irish immigrant gets a job as a waiter at West Point Military Academy. He becomes a cadet and marries an Irish immigrant housekeeper. He continues his post at West Point as athletic trainer for fifty years, helping to train men for combat in both world wars. This film is based on a true story.

THEME—Dedication to country and freedom outweighs hardships and heartaches.

FAVORITE SCENE—On the first Christmas after his wife's death, Marty Maher (Power) is overcome with emotion when some of the cadets show up to cook him breakfast. Kitty Sundstrom (Palmer) and her son, James (Francis), arrive with a tree and James's captain's badge, which he asks Marty to pin onto him.

MEMORABLE LINES—Marty pins James Redstone Sr.'s ribbon next to his photo in the yearbook after he learns of his death. "The finest young men in the world. We bring 'em here, train them, teach them duty, honor, and country, and then send them out to be killed."

TAKE NOTE—John Ford directed 131 movies, half of them silent films, over a period of 49 years.

TRIVIA QUIZ—What is so unusual about Marty being a swimming instructor to the cadets? (Answer No. 56)

> *Nine times out of ten, the best thing that can happen to a young man is to be tossed overboard and compelled to sink or swim.*
>
> —JAMES A. GARFIELD

68

The Long Hot Summer
Drama/Romance 1958

Director: Martin Ritt

Starring: Paul Newman, Joanne Woodward, Orson Welles, Anthony Franciosa, Lee Remick, Angela Lansbury, Richard Anderson

●●●●●●●●●●●●●●●●●●●●●●●●●●●●●●●●●●

STORY CONCEPT—A stranger arrives in Frenchman's Bend, a town owned by one man who has an unmarried daughter. The outsider promotes himself quickly and goes from tenant farmer to landowner, and eventually becomes a prospective husband for the daughter who is reluctant to have him.

THEME—Love without passion is plodding.

FAVORITE SCENE—Clara (Woodward), the unmarried school-teacher, enters the store where Ben Quick (Newman) is working late. She slaps him when he comes on too strong. He kisses her and she kisses him back. Feeling guilty about it, she insults him by calling him a barnburner, something his father had been.

MEMORABLE LINES—Ben and Clara discuss their relationship.

Clara: I've got a lot to give—love, friendship, fun. I'm not going to give it to any passing stranger.
Ben: All right then, run, lady—and you keep on running. Buy yourself a bus ticket and disappear. Change your name, dye your hair, get lost, and then maybe, just maybe, you're gonna be safe from me.

TAKE NOTE—Newman and Woodward, who were paired together for the first time in this movie, also got married in the same year.

TRIVIA QUIZ—Who does Clara say Ben Quick reminds her of? (Answer No. 57)

People who never get carried away should be.
                                        —MALCOLM FORBES
None are so old as those who have outlived enthusiasm.
                                        —HENRY DAVID THOREAU

Man of a Thousand Faces

Biography/Drama 1957

Director: Joseph Pevney

Starring: James Cagney, Dorothy Malone, Jane Greer, Jim Backus

●●●●●●●●●●●●●●●●●●●●●●●●●●●●●●●●●●●●●●

STORY CONCEPT—A son, whose parents are deaf and mute, is a master of make-up and has a successful career in silent movies. Based on a true story.

THEME—An unusual childhood can provide a training ground for an unusual profession.

FAVORITE SCENE—Cleva (Malone), Lon Chaney's (Cagney) new pregnant wife, meets his parents for the first time. She is so upset to learn they are deaf mutes that she runs from the dinner table, visualizing that her unborn child may end up the same.

MEMORABLE LINES—Lon and Hazel Bennet (Greer) discuss his predicament with his son who has been in foster care for several years because the judge refuses to let Lon care for him.

Hazel: Lon, I was just thinking, maybe a suitable home doesn't mean just a house and furniture. The judge may mean people—a father, mother—you know, people.
Lon: Tell you what, tomorrow on the extra ad sheet I'm gonna put an ad in the paper: Wanted, one mother type, under fifty, to fall in love with actor and son.
Hazel: I'm under fifty, Lon.

TAKE NOTE—Lon Chaney made 155 movies, all silent but one. After his first talking picture, *The Unholy Three*, he got cancer of the throat and became mute like his parents.

TRIVIA QUIZ—What are Lon Chaney's two most famous films? (Answer No. 58)

A man's doubts and fears are his worst enemies.

—WILLIAM WRIGLEY, JR.

Marty

Drama/Romance 1955

Director: Delbert Mann

Starring: Ernest Borgnine, Betsy Blair, Esther Minciotti, Joe Mantell

• •

STORY CONCEPT—A lonely, middle-aged butcher meets and finds happiness with a schoolteacher, in spite of his mother, other relatives, and friends who try to run his life.

THEME—A yearning for love can be resurrected, even when time and circumstances have buried it.

FAVORITE SCENE—Marty (Borgnine) meets Clara (Blair) for the first time at the Stardust Ballroom. Her date offers Marty five dollars if he'll take her home. He refuses, but another fellow takes the money and tells Clara what has transpired. Heartbroken, she runs from the ballroom. Marty follows her out and comforts her.

MEMORABLE LINES—Angie (Mantell) expresses how he feels about Marty's new friend, Clara. Marty responds, "All I know is I had a good time last night. If we have enough good times together, I'm going to get down on my knees. I'm going to beg that girl to marry me. (Pause) You don't like her? That's too bad!"

TAKE NOTE—*Marty* was first shown as a TV play. It was successful and opened the door to other plays being adapted for the movies. Ernest Borgnine, a 40-year-old character actor, got his first chance in this movie to break away from his "bad guy" roles. He received an Academy Award for his efforts.

TRIVIA QUIZ—Why did Marty's mother, Mrs. Piletti (Minciotti), discourage Marty from seeing Clara? (Answer No. 59)

> *The U.S. Constitution doesn't guarantee happiness, only the pursuit of it. You have to catch up with it yourself.*
>
> —BENJAMIN FRANKLIN

Miracle on 34th Street

Comedy/Fantasy 1947

Director: George Seaton

Starring: Maureen O'Hara, John Payne, Edmund Gwenn, Natalie Wood, Gene Lockhart, Jerome Cowan, Bobby Hyatt

● ●

STORY CONCEPT—Macy's Santa gets drunk and is replaced by Kris Kringle, who claims to be the real Santa Claus. A quack psychiatrist proclaims Kringle insane and a trial ensues to prove whether or not he's the real Santa.

THEME—Everyone needs faith in someone or something.

FAVORITE SCENE—Kris Kringle (Gwenn) tells prospective customers to buy their gifts in competitive stores. People are amazed as they take their children through the line to see this Santa. They praise his unusual business practice.

MEMORABLE LINES—Fred Galey (Payne) brings young Thomas (Hyatt), the son of the prosecuting attorney (Cowan), to the witness stand during Kringle's trial.

Galey: Do you believe in Santa Claus?
Thomas: (Nods and points to Kris Kringle.)
Galey: Why do you believe in Santa?
Thomas: Because my daddy told me so! (Looking at his father who drops his head while the courtroom erupts in laughter.)

TAKE NOTE—Edmund Gwenn, who starred as Kris Kringle, actually played Santa in the real Macy's Thanksgiving Day parade.

TRIVIA QUIZ—What finally settles the case for the defense in the trial against Kris Kringle? (Answer No. 60)

> *If a man practices doing things for other people until it becomes so much a habit that he is unconscious of it, all the good forces of the universe will line up behind him and whatever he undertakes to do.* —BRUCE BARTON

Mister Roberts
Comedy/Drama 1955

Directors: John Ford and Mervyn LeRoy

Starring: Henry Fonda, James Cagney, Jack Lemmon,
William Powell, Betsy Palmer

● ●

STORY CONCEPT—A naval lieutenant seeks to gain his freedom from the tyrannical captain of a cargo ship and gets transferred to a battle ship.

THEME—Courage is recognized and rewarded for mundane service as well as for hard-fought battles.

FAVORITE SCENE—Ensign Pulver (Lemmon) staggers into the presence of Doc (Powell) and Mr. Roberts (Fonda) after testing a homemade firecracker that he plans to put under the captain's (Cagney) bunk. The explosion in the laundry room rocks the whole ship. Serious-minded Mr. Roberts laughs uncontrollably when he sees Pulver covered in soapsuds.

MEMORABLE LINES—Ensign Pulver reads a letter from Mr. Roberts to the crew: "All the guys who sailed from tedium to apathy and back again with an occasional trip to monotony have discovered that the unseen enemy of this war is the boredom that eventually becomes a fate and a terrible form of suicide. I know now that the ones who refuse to surrender to it are the strongest of all."

TAKE NOTE—James Cagney, who plays the tough captain, was honored at a banquet in 1974, where he gave thanks for "that touch of the gutter" in his hard-times youth without which, he said, his career would not have been possible.

TRIVIA QUIZ—What is the name of the cargo ship? (Answer No. 61)

> *Nobody makes the greater mistake than he who did nothing because he could only do a little.* —EDMUND BURKE

My Darling Clementine
Western 1946

Director: John Ford

Starring: Henry Fonda, Victor Mature, Cathy Downs, Walter Brennan, Linda Darnell, Ward Bond, Tim Holt, John Ireland

● ●

STORY CONCEPT—Wyatt Earp (Fonda) takes the job as sheriff in the Wild West town of Tombstone, Arizona, where he meets Doc Holliday (Mature), a gambler, gunfighter, and ex-surgeon, who becomes his ally in a showdown with the Clantons.

THEME—The search for justice demands sacrifice and teamwork.

FAVORITE SCENE—Clementine Carter (Downs) is ready to leave Tombstone and Doc Holliday when she meets Marshall Wyatt Earp in the town's hotel lobby. She invites the shy Wyatt to a church social where he asks her to dance. This leads to her decision to stay in Tombstone as the new schoolmarm.

MEMORABLE LINES—Wyatt at the gravesite of his youngest brother James, who was killed by cattle rustlers: "You didn't get much of a chance did you, James? I'll be coming out regular to see you, James. So will Morg and Virg. I'm gonna be around here for a while. Can't tell. Maybe when we leave this country, young kids like you will be able to grow up and live safe."

TAKE NOTE—Director John Ford knew the real Wyatt Earp. He based this story on his recollection that Earp had confessed to him about being a poor shot with a gun.

TRIVIA QUIZ—Why did Clementine go to Tombstone? (Answer No. 62)

> *Everyone has it within his power to say, this I am today, that I shall be tomorrow.* — LOUIS L'AMOUR

National Velvet

Drama 1944

Director: Clarence Brown

Starring: Mickey Rooney, Elizabeth Taylor, Anne Revere, Donald Crisp, Angela Lansbury, Jackie "Butch" Jenkins

• •

STORY CONCEPT—A twelve-year-old English girl who loves horses meets an eighteen-year-old ex-jockey and trainer who trains her new horse, Pi, for the Grand National Steeplechase. When a newly hired jockey loses faith in the horse, the English girl disguises herself as a male and rides Pi herself.

THEME—Dreams really do come true for youth with the help of a mother and a friend.

FAVORITE SCENE—Mrs. Brown (Revere) takes her daughter, Velvet (Taylor), to the attic and shows her a trunk of memories—a trophy, a scrapbook, and one hundred gold sovereigns that she won for being the first woman to swim the English Channel. Velvet's mother gives her the money to enter Pi in the steeplechase.

MEMORABLE LINES—Velvet's father (Crisp) talks of selling Pi.

Velvet: The Pi is too wonderful, noble and great!
Mi Taylor (Rooney): Great? Someday you'll learn that greatness is only the seizing of opportunity, clutching it with your bare hands 'til the knuckles show white.

TAKE NOTE—This was Elizabeth Taylor's first starring role, at age twelve.

TRIVIA QUIZ—What is the link between Mi Taylor and Mrs. Brown? (Answer No. 63)

> *All dreams do not come true. Only dreams that are dreamed come true. So dream anyway!* —GYNNATH FORD

The Night of the Hunter
Thriller 1955

Director: Charles Laughton

Starring: Robert Mitchum, Shelley Winters, Lillian Gish, Billy Chapin

• •

STORY CONCEPT—An ex-con preacher marries the widow of an executed cellmate in order to find the money he hid from a bank robbery. He kills the widow and threatens her offspring who run away with the money. A woman befriends the children and takes them in to protect them from the evil preacher.

THEME—Good triumphs over evil.

FAVORITE SCENE—"Preacher" Harry Powell (Mitchum) marries Willa Harper (Winters). On their wedding night, he accuses her of immoral sexual feelings and demands that she look in the mirror to see herself as the sinner she is. He fervently believes that sex is only for producing children and she wants no more children; therefore there will be no sex between them.

MEMORABLE LINES—Rachel Cooper (Gish), who cares for children of the Depression, sits on her front porch shielding the two Harper children from Powell. She watches an owl attack a helpless rabbit. Alluding to the helpless children she protects, she says to herself, "It's a hard world for little things."

TAKE NOTE—This film, which has become a classic, was the only movie Charles Laughton directed. He became discouraged with its lack of success at the box office.

TRIVIA QUIZ—What does Pearl Harper do with the stolen money that's hidden in her doll? (Answer No. 64)

> *Beware of false prophets which come to you in sheep's clothing, but inwardly they are ravening wolves. You shall know them by their fruits.* —JESUS

A Night to Remember

Drama 1958

Director: Roy Ward Baker

Starring: Kenneth More, Laurence Naismith, Michael Goodliffe, Honor Blackman, David McCallum

• •

STORY CONCEPT—The sinking of the *Titanic* follows 2nd Officer Charles H. Lightoller (More), one of the survivors, from the time he leaves his wife in England until he is rescued.

THEME—Human neglect and vanity are the source of much tragedy.

FAVORITE SCENE—The dispatcher of the *Titanic* frantically sends SOS messages to the *Californian,* whose dispatcher has retired for the night.

MEMORABLE LINES—Thomas Andrews (Goodliffe), an architect, confers with Captain Smith (Naismith) about how little time there is before the ship sinks.

Andrews: How many people on the boat?
Smith: Two thousand, two hundred and eight.
Andrews: How many will the lifeboats hold?
Smith: Twelve hundred. (There is silence and look of disbelief on their faces.)

TAKE NOTE—The captain of the *Californian,* which was ten miles away when the *Titanic* went under, is rumored not to have enjoyed the film because it's believed that he and his crew ignored the calls for help from the *Titanic.*

TRIVIA QUIZ—Why is the crew not more alert to the danger of the icebergs? (Answer No. 65)

Pride goes before destruction, and a haughty spirit before a fall.
—THE BIBLE

No Highway in the Sky
Drama 1951

Director: Henry Koster

Starring: James Stewart, Marlene Dietrich, Glynis Johns, Jack Hawkins

● ●

STORY CONCEPT—An absent-minded scientist conducts an experiment he believes will prove that Britain's new Reindeer airplane will lose its tail after 1440 hours of flight. On a flight to Labrador to investigate a plane crash, he learns that the Reindeer plane he's on has been airborne for a total of 1422 hours. He warns the pilot and passengers of their impending doom.

THEME—One who is convinced he holds the truth should put action behind his words.

FAVORITE SCENE—Scientist Theodore Honey (Stewart) tells the stewardess, Ms. Corder (Johns), and one of the passengers that the safest place to sit during a plane crash is the floor of the men's room. They eye him with suspicion.

MEMORABLE LINES—Mr. Honey is in the custody of Ms. Corder after he pulls the lever in the plane that causes it to collapse.

Mr. Honey: I can't imagine what the Establishment will think. I suppose I better let them know what I've done.
Ms. Corder: I imagine they'll hear about it. Man Kills Airplane. There'll be quite a bit in the newspaper about that.

TAKE NOTE—James Stewart, an aircraft enthusiast, joined the army in 1941 after stuffing himself with fattening food so he could pass the weight test. He passed by one ounce.

TRIVIA QUIZ—How does Ms. Corder intend to take care of Mr. Honey? (Answer No. 66)

> *When you have decided what you believe, what you feel must be done, have the courage to stand alone and be counted.*
>
> —ELEANOR ROOSEVELT

North by Northwest
Thriller/Drama 1959

Director: Alfred Hitchcock

Starring: Cary Grant, Eva Marie Saint, James Mason, Leo G. Carroll, Martin Landau, Jessie Royce Landis

● ●

STORY CONCEPT—An advertising executive is mistaken for a government agent and is chased across the country by both spies and the law.

THEME—The desire for survival motivates a man to take chances beyond what he normally would take.

FAVORITE SCENE—Roger Thornhill (Grant) finds himself in the midwest plains after stepping off the bus at an isolated location. A crop-dusting plane appears and shots ring out. Roger, realizing his life is in jeopardy and that the plane is to "dust him off," runs for his life. He drops to the ground and looks up to see the plane crashing into a fuel tanker truck driving down the highway.

MEMORABLE LINES—Roger and an attractive lady strike up a conversation after meeting in the dining car of a train. Eve Kendall (Saint) shows an above-average interest in him.

Eve: My problem is I'm always meeting men who don't believe in marriage.
Roger: Not me. I've been married twice!
Eve: See what I mean!

TAKE NOTE—Director Hitchcock wanted Grant to have a sneezing fit on the nose of Lincoln (Mt. Rushmore), but the U.S. government would not permit it. They didn't want anyone playing around with such a sacred monument, much less Lincoln's nose.

TRIVIA QUIZ—What is the one thing Alfred Hitchcock does in all of his movies? (Answer No. 67)

But screw your courage to the sticking place and we'll not fail.
—WILLIAM SHAKESPEARE

The Nun's Story
Drama 1959

Director: Fred Zinnemann

Starring: Audrey Hepburn, Peter Finch, Dame Edith Evans, Dean Jagger

● ●

STORY CONCEPT—A strong-willed doctor's daughter chooses a career as a nurse and a vocation as a nun over married life. She reaches her life's goal when she becomes a nun and a nurse in the Congo, but still has a conflict in her mind about God's plan for her.

THEME—The call to serve God does not override the personal choice as to how this is best done.

FAVORITE SCENE—Sister Luke's (Hepburn) superior asks her to fail a test so that a missionary nun will feel equal. This goes against all she's been taught, but obedience to authority (not her strength) wins out.

MEMORABLE LINES—An African helper asks Sister Luke about her life.

Helper: I don't understand why you don't have a husband.
Sister Luke: I do have a husband, but he's in heaven.
Helper (thinking her husband must be dead): I'm sorry.

TAKE NOTE—Audrey Hepburn, who died at age 63, spent the last years of her life, while working for the United Nations Children's Fund, visiting refugee camps in Africa and Asia.

TRIVIA QUIZ—Why were nuns medically less qualified sent to Africa while Sister Luke remained in Europe? (Answer No. 68)

Never say never. Never is a long undependable thing, and life is too full of rich possibilities to have restrictions placed upon it.
—GLORIA SWANSON

Our Vines Have Tender Grapes

Drama 1945

Director: Roy Rowland

Starring: Edward G. Robinson, Margaret O'Brien,
Jackie "Butch" Jenkins, Agnes Moorehead,
Francis Gifford, James Craig

• •

STORY CONCEPT—A seven-year-old girl in rural Wisconsin learns to face the challenge of personal loss with a mature attitude.

THEME—Children who are nurtured in a favorable environment excel in character.

FAVORITE SCENE—After church services, the local newspaper editor, Nels Haverson (Craig), makes an appeal to the congregation to assist in helping Bjorn Bjornson whose barn and cows were destroyed in a fire. Only a few dollars are contributed, but seven-year-old Selma Jacobson (O'Brien) offers her young calf. Others then generously give their pigs, cows, calves, and feed.

MEMORABLE LINES—Martinius Jacobson (Robinson) and his daughter, Selma, talk after seeing their neighbor's new barn.

Selma: Do you want a new barn, Pa?
Robinson: Every man wants a new barn.
Selma: Then I'll pray for one.
Robinson: Selma, that's fine. That'll take considerable praying.
Selma: What's one more barn to God!

TAKE NOTE—Robinson, who appeared in over 80 movies, playing mostly tough-guy roles, acted as a kind and loving father in this film.

TRIVIA QUIZ—What gift did young Arnold (Jenkins), Selma's neighbor, give to her for Christmas? (Answer No. 69)

Children are poor men's riches.—ANONYMOUS

Out of the Past

Drama 1947

Director: Jacques Tourneur

Starring: Robert Mitchum, Kirk Douglas, Jane Greer, Rhonda Fleming, Steve Brodie

● ●

STORY CONCEPT—A private detective double-crosses a gambler who's hired him to find an ex-girlfriend. After falling in love with this femme fatale, the detective is blamed for a murder that she committed and she deserts him. He changes his name but ten years later his past catches up with him.

THEME—Men should consider the wiles of beautiful women before they come to ruin.

FAVORITE SCENE—Private Detective Jeff Markham (Mitchum) sees Kathy Moffet (Greer), the lady he was hired to find, for the first time and understands why gambler Whit Sterling (Douglas) doesn't care about the forty grand that was stolen from him.

MEMORABLE LINES—Whit Sterling meets up with Markham, who is now Jeff Bailey, ten years after he was double-crossed.

Sterling: I understand you're operating a little gas station.
Markham: You say it like it was hard to understand.
Sterling: It is.
Markham: It's very simple. I sell gas, make a small profit. I buy groceries; the grocer makes a profit. They call it earning a living. You may have heard of it somewhere.

TAKE NOTE –Greer's first starring role was in *Out of the Past*. This movie was remade 37 years later as *Against All Odds* with Jane Greer cast as the mother of the femme fatale.

TRIVIA QUIZ—What fatal mistake does Whit Sterling make in this film? (Answer No. 70)

Those who cannot remember the past are condemned to repeat it.

—GEORGE SANTAYANA

People Will Talk
Romantic Comedy 1951

Director: Joseph L. Mankiewicz

Starring: Cary Grant, Jeanne Crain, Finlay Currie,
Sidney Blackner, Walter Slezak, Hume Cronyn

● ●

STORY CONCEPT—A successful, yet unorthodox doctor is scrutinized by a fellow professor for his practices as well as for his relationship with an unwed mother and a mysterious assistant who is always by his side.

THEME—Often times, losers will try to pull you down to their level.

FAVORITE SCENE—Dr. Noah Praetorius (Grant) and his assistant, Shunderson (Currie), pay a visit to Deborah Huggins (Crain) at her father's farm where she is embarrassed and overcome by the guilt she feels about her pregnancy and attempted suicide.

MEMORABLE LINES—In Dr. Noah's office, after a fainting spell, where the doctor is examining Deborah.

Dr. Noah: Mrs. Higgins, you have nothing to worry about.
Deborah: The fainting, that's not abnormal?
Dr. Noah: Get the receptionist to give you another appointment in about a month.
Deborah: Didn't you say I have nothing to worry about?
Dr. Noah: Yes, you're pregnant. (Deborah breaks down.) You're not married, are you?

TAKE NOTE—This movie especially appealed to Cary Grant who fought hard against the inefficiency of conventional medicine and was an advocate of health foods long before they became fashionable.

TRIVIA QUIZ—What was Cary Grant's reply to an interviewer who said, "Everyone would like to be Cary Grant?" (Answer No. 71)

If everybody is thinking alike, somebody isn't thinking.

—GENERAL GEORGE PATTON

Pinky

Drama 1949

Director: Elia Kazan

Starring: Jeanne Crain, Ethel Waters, Ethel Barrymore, William Lundigan, Evelyn Varden

● ●

STORY CONCEPT—A young mulatto woman from the South, in nursing training in Boston, becomes engaged to a white doctor. When she gets second thoughts about marrying him and returns home, he follows hoping to win her back.

THEME—It is better to accept one's past and move on than try to escape it.

FAVORITE SCENE—A greedy relative (Varden) visits wealthy Miss Em (Barrymore) while Pinky (Crain) attends to her. The relative protests too loudly about Pinky's position as a nurse and loses the debate with a bedridden but humorous Miss Em.

MEMORABLE LINES—Dr. Tom Adams (Lundigan) pleads with Pinky to return to Boston.

Tom: You can change your name and become Mrs. Thomas Adams.
Pinky: You can change your name, but I wonder if you can really change who you are inside for the rest of your life.

TAKE NOTE—This movie was well received in the segregated south. In Atlanta, the allotment of balcony seats for blacks was increased for the showing of this film.

TRIVIA QUIZ—In the film, what first establishes Pinky as a black woman? (Answer No. 72)

Life can only be understood backwards, but it must be lived forward. —SOREN KIERKEGAARD

The Quiet Man

Romantic Comedy 1952

Director: John Ford

Starring: John Wayne, Maureen O'Hara, Barry Fitzgerald,
Victor McLaglen, Ward Bond

● ●

STORY CONCEPT—An Irish-American boxer moves to Ireland after accidentally killing a fighter in the ring. In his homeland, he falls in love with and marries the beautiful sister of a bully who belittles him because he's afraid to fight. The sister, thinking that he's a coward, tries to leave him.

THEME—Fear of loss awakens one to their responsibility as a human being.

FAVORITE SCENE—Sean Thornton (Wayne) pulls his wife, Mary Kate (O'Hara), off the train and drags her back to her brother's (McLaglen) farm where he demands her dowry or the marriage is over. Sean and her brother have the fight of the century.

MEMORABLE LINES—When Mary Kate's furniture is brought to the house the day after their wedding, Sean shows no interest in her dowry of money that her brother keeps. Maloney, their security guard, is nearby.

Mary Kate: It's my money!
Sean: Let him have it if it means that much to him. (He walks away.)
Mary Kate: What manner of man is it that I have married?
Maloney: A better one, I think, than you know, Mary Kate.

TAKE NOTE—Filmed in breathtaking Ireland, the movie wins the Academy Award for Best Cinematography, and Best Director for Ford, his fourth. O'Hara is one of the few stars who was not overshadowed by the presence of John Wayne in a movie.

TRIVIA QUIZ—What does Sean Thornton do with the dowry that Mary Kate's brother gives to him? (Answer No. 73)

A mountain man tries to live with the country instead of against it. —LOUIS L'AMOUR

Random Harvest

Romance 1942

Director: Mervyn LeRoy

Starring: Ronald Coleman, Greer Garson, Susan Peters

• •

STORY CONCEPT—At the end of World War I, a soldier with amnesia wanders out of an asylum. He meets a singer and marries her. While working for a newspaper, he's hit by a car and regains some of his memory, so he goes back to his former life as a wealthy industrialist. His wife gets a job as his secretary in the hopes that his memory of her also will return.

THEME—Unrequited love requires great faith and patience.

FAVORITE SCENE—Sir Charles Ranier (Coleman) and Kitty (Peters), his fiancé, are selecting their wedding music when he recalls the music that was played at his first marriage ceremony with Paula (Garson). This incident causes Kitty to cancel their wedding plans.

MEMORABLE LINES—Sir Charles asks Paula, his secretary, to be his wife.

Sir Charles: You and I are in the same boat. We are both ghost-driven. We are prisoners of our past.
Paula: Yes.
Sir Charles: What if we were to pool our loneliness and give each other what we have to give—support, friendship—and form a merger? I'd be lost without you. (Paula is silent, almost in tears.)

TAKE NOTE—Coleman was 53 years old when he portrayed the 29-year-old character in this film.

TRIVIA QUIZ—What is Sir Charles' only clue to his past life when he regains his memory? (Answer No. 74)

There is no medicine like hope, no incentive so great, and no tonic so powerful as expectation of something tomorrow.

—ORISON SWETT MARDEN

Rear Window
Thriller/Romance 1954

Director: Alfred Hitchcock

Starring: Jimmy Stewart, Grace Kelly, Thelma Ritter, Wendell Corey, Raymond Burr

● ●

STORY CONCEPT—A society beauty loves a photographer who attempts to talk her out of marriage while he is laid up with his leg in a cast. From the large rear window of his apartment he views people in adjoining apartments and suspects a man has murdered his wife. He cannot investigate personally, so he enlists the help of his eager girlfriend and the police who have no evidence to follow.

THEME—You sometimes see the faults of others when you will not see your own.

FAVORITE SCENE—Lisa Freemont (Kelly) gets into the suspect's room and is searching for clues to a murder when the suspect opens the door and surprises her. L. B. Jeffries (Stewart) is watching from his apartment and can do nothing to warn her.

MEMORABLE LINES—Stella (Ritter), Jeffries' maid, rebukes him: "We've become a race of Peeping Toms. What people ought to do is get outside their own house and look in for a change. Yes sir. How's that for a bit of homespun philosophy?"

TAKE NOTE—In 1954, this movie set was the largest indoor set built at Paramount Studios and every scene was shot from inside the Jeffries' apartment, giving the viewer of the movie the same impressions Jeffries experiences.

TRIVIA QUIZ—What book is Lisa reading at the conclusion of the movie, and what magazine does she exchange it for when she sees L. B. has fallen asleep? (Answer No. 75)

> *The moment someone says 'this is very risky' it becomes attractive to me.* —KATE CAPSHAW

Roman Holiday

Comedy/Romance 1953

Director: William Wyler

Starring: Audrey Hepburn, Gregory Peck, Eddie Albert

● ●

STORY CONCEPT—A lonely princess visiting Rome decides her life is too restricted and runs away for a day. She meets an American reporter who serves as her guide, and they fall for each other.

THEME—A life of nobility forfeits freedoms others take for granted.

FAVORITE SCENE—Princess Anne (Hepburn), Joe Bradley (Peck), the reporter, and Irving Radovich (Albert), the photographer, visit the grotesque statue of truth. Joe warns Princess Anne that if she puts her hand in the mouth of the creature and tells the truth she will not be harmed. She is reluctant, but Joe thrusts his hand in and pulls it out quickly. She squeals with fright because she can't see his hand.

MEMORABLE LINES—In an interview with Princess Anne by reporters after her day of fun in Rome with Bradley:

Reporter: And what, in the opinion of Your Highness, is the outlook for a friendship among nations?
Princess: I have every faith in it—as I have faith in relations between people.
Bradley: May I say, speaking for my own (pause) press service, we believe Your Highness's faith will not be unjustified.
Princess: I am so glad to hear you say it. (She smiles with relief as Irving hands her the photographs he had taken.)

TAKE NOTE—The scene in which Peck pretends that his hand is bitten off in the mouth of the statue was ad-libbed, and Hepburn's response was genuine.

TRIVIA QUIZ—Who won an Oscar in this film in their first leading role? (Answer No. 76)

Enjoying each other's good is heaven begun. —LUCY C. SMITH

Separate Tables

Drama 1958

Director: Delbert Mann

Starring: Deborah Kerr, David Niven, Rita Hayworth, Burt Lancaster, Wendy Hiller, Gladys Cooper

● ●

STORY CONCEPT—A group of lonely and frustrated people residing at a seaside hotel confront and befriend each other, and explore their futures.

THEME—Loneliness is more a matter of insulation than isolation.

FAVORITE SCENE —Major Pollock (Niven) plans to leave the hotel because of the publicity surrounding his sexual indiscretion. That morning, in the dining room, shy Sibyl (Kerr) disobeys her mother (Cooper) and refuses to leave the breakfast table because of her concern for the major.

MEMORABLE LINES—Mrs. Raiton-Bell calls for a vote from all the guests except her daughter, Sibyl, regarding Major Pollock and asking him to leave. When John Malcolm (Lancaster) asks for her opinion, Sibyl breaks down and is escorted from the room by her mother. Malcolm remarks, "I thought I might get her once to publicly disagree with her mother. It would save her soul if she did."

TAKE NOTE—Sir Lawrence Olivier and his wife, Vivian Leigh, were originally signed to direct and co-star in this film.

TRIVIA QUIZ—Where did the movie get its title? (Answer No. 77)

Nothing is a greater impediment to being on good terms with others than being ill at ease with yourself.

—HONORE DE BALZAC

Sergeant York

Drama/War 1941

Director: Howard Hawks

Starring: Gary Cooper, Joan Leslie, Walter Brennan, Margaret Wycherly, George Tobias, Ward Bond

● ●

STORY CONCEPT—True story of a shy farmer from Tennessee who serves in World War II as a conscientious objector and becomes the greatest recruited war hero.

THEME—The use of violence to ensure peace and freedom is not easily discerned.

FAVORITE SCENE—Sergeant Alvin York (Cooper), an expert sharpshooter, is questioned by Major Buxton (Stanley Ridges) about his unwillingness to defend his country. The major doesn't argue, but loans him a history book of the United States and asks why Daniel Boone explored the wilderness. The answer is freedom. After reading the book, York begins to see freedom in a new light.

MEMORABLE LINES—Alvin visits neighbor Gracie Williams (Leslie) and finds her talking to Zeb Andrews (Robert Porterfield).

Alvin: Ms. Gracie, I would be pleased to have some water.
Gracie: How about some cider. (While she's gone Alvin takes Zeb out into the woods and gives him a thrashing.)
Gracie (upon returning): Where's Zeb?
Alvin: He ain't coming back.
Gracie: Why not?
Alvin: 'Cause I'm gonna marry you! (They begin to argue.)

TAKE NOTE—Alvin C. York, who single-handedly captured 132 prisoners, was a consultant on this film.

TRIVIA QUIZ—What would Sergeant York do to get a wild turkey's attention? (Answer No. 78)

A twinge of conscience is a glimpse of God. —PETER USTINOV

Shadow of a Doubt
Thriller 1943

Director: Alfred Hitchcock

Starring: Teresa Wright, Joseph Cotten, MacDonald Carey, Patricia Collinge, Henry Travers, Hume Cronyn

• •

STORY CONCEPT—A young lady seeks to liven up her dull life by requesting her city-dweller uncle to visit. His mysterious past and strange ways make life more lively than she imagined, as the evidence begins to mount that proves him to be the murderer of two widows.

THEME—Doubt leads to close scrutiny, which brings about certainty.

FAVORITE SCENE—Young Charlie (Wright) wonders why Uncle Charlie (Cotten) has torn an article out of the newspaper. She rushes to the library to check it out and finds out that a man has been murdering rich widows for their money and that the name of one of the victims is on the beautiful ring Uncle Charlie gave to her.

MEMORABLE LINES—Uncle Charlie to young Charlie when she confronts him with her discovery: "You think you know something, don't you? . . . There's so much you don't know. So much. What do you know really? You're just an ordinary little girl living in an ordinary little town. You go through your ordinary little day, and, at night, you sleep your untroubled, ordinary little sleep filled with peaceful stupid dreams. And I brought you nightmares."

TAKE NOTE—Alfred Hitchcock named the character of the mother, Emma Newton (played by Patricia Collinge), after his own mother who was dying in war-torn England at the time.

TRIVIA QUIZ—What's the favorite pastime of Mr. Newton (Travers), young Charlie's father, and Herbie Hawkins (Cronyn)? (Answer No. 79)

The darkest hour of any man's life is when he sits down to plan how to get money without earning it. —HORACE GREELEY

Shane
Western 1953

Director: George Stevens

Starring: Alan Ladd, Jean Arthur, Van Heflin, Brandon De Wilde, Jack Palance, Ben Johnson

● ●

STORY CONCEPT—Shane (Ladd) is a retired gunfighter who comes to the aid of a homestead family terrorized by a cattle baron and his hired gun.

THEME—The decent life, though difficult, can be admired by those who have given their lives to unworthy ventures.

FAVORITE SCENE—The first night Shane stays with Joe (Heflin), Mariam (Arthur), and their son, Joey (DeWilde), he envies their lifestyle and Joey is captivated by him. The parents see a difficulty here because they want Joey to live a non-violent life unlike the life of Shane.

MEMORABLE LINES—Shane to Ryker, the wicked cattle baron:

Shane: Your kind of days are over.
Ryker: My days! What about yours, gunfighter?
Shane: The difference is I know it!

TAKE NOTE—Jack Palance, who plays the hired gunfighter, did not like horses. He only mounted a horse well one time in the movie and that scene was not used. The part where he walks his horse into town the first time was not originally planned that way, but due to his noticeably unsteady riding manner, the director kept it in the film. It has become a classic scene in movie history.

TRIVIA QUIZ—What unpopular drink for gunfighters does Shane order at the bar? (Answer No. 80)

I fear there will be no future for those who do not change.
—LOUIS L'AMOUR

We run away all the time to avoid coming face to face with ourselves. —ANONYMOUS

The Shop Around the Corner

Romantic Comedy 1940

Director: Ernst Lubitsch

Starring: James Stewart, Margaret Sullavan, Frank Morgan, Joseph Schildkraut

● ●

STORY CONCEPT—A man and a woman working together in a gift shop in Budapest, Hungary, each have a secret pen pal. The two employees, who don't get along at all, have no idea that they are pen pals with each other.

THEME—Writing down your true feelings is sometimes easier than saying them aloud to another person.

FAVORITE SCENE—Alfred Kralik (Stewart) misses an appointment to meet his pen pal because he has to work late. His boss, Mr. Matuschek (Morgan), fires him because he thinks Kralik is having an affair with his wife. Depressed, Kalik asks an associate to take a note to his pen pal, Klara (Sullavan).

MEMORABLE LINES—Kralik talks to Klara in a café as if it were by chance, even though he knows that she's his pen pal. She has no clue.

Kralik: You may have beautiful thoughts, but you certainly hide them. You'll have a tough time getting a man to fall in love with you.
Klara: The letters I receive are written by a man of such superior intelligence to you it isn't even funny, you little insignificant clerk.

TAKE NOTE—Ernst Lubitsch, a director known for his elegant comedies, had the practice of acting out all the roles for all the actors, from bit players to the stars.

TRIVIA QUIZ—What movie released in 1998 has a similar story line? (Answer No. 81)

The difference between the right word and the almost right word is the difference between lightning and the lightning bug.

—MARK TWAIN

Spellbound

Thriller/Romance 1945

Director: Alfred Hitchcock

Starring: Ingrid Bergman, Gregory Peck, Leo G. Carroll, Rhonda Fleming

• •

STORY CONCEPT—A doctor believes he murdered another doctor. In the guise of the deceased, he becomes the head of a mental hospital where a lady psychiatrist guides him in finding out the truth, and they fall in love.

THEME—Guilt and denial in a person's mind are sometimes difficult to unravel.

FAVORITE SCENE—After a picnic with Edwardes (Peck), Constance (Bergman) cannot sleep and goes to the library where she gets a copy of his new book. She sees a light on under Edwardes door and finds him dozing inside. He wakes up and smiles at her.

MEMORABLE LINES—Dr. Peterson awakens Edwardes.

Dr. Peterson: I thought I wanted to discuss your book with you, but it was a subterfuge.
Dr. Edwardes: I know why you came in.
Dr. Peterson: Why?
Dr. Edwardes: Because something has happened to us. (They embrace and kiss.)

TAKE NOTE—Ingrid Bergman didn't want to do the movie at first because she didn't buy the love story. Throughout filming, she voiced her objections to Director Hitchcock who sat quietly and replied sweetly, "Fake it."

TRIVIA QUIZ—When Bergman and Peck kiss, an image of four doors opening one after the other is seen. What does this represent? (Answer No. 82)

> *The mind is an instrument, which plays many melodies and needs frequent tuning.* —GYNNATH FORD

94

The Spirit of St. Louis

Biography 1957

Director: Billy Wilder

Starring: James Stewart, Murray Hamilton, Patricia Smith, Marc Connelly

● ●

STORY CONCEPT—The true story of hero Charles Lindbergh and the first transatlantic flight in a single-engine plane built especially for this daring adventure.

THEME—Confidence, courage, and experience are a great trio to travel with in untried territory.

FAVORITE SCENE—Lindbergh's (Stewart) takeoff in mud and rain takes the help of ten men. He barely misses the trees and drags an electrical wire up into the air with him.

MEMORABLE LINES—Before supporting Lindbergh's venture, he is questioned by a bank president in St. Louis concerning his qualifications.

Bank president: How do you know you can fly a plane to Paris?
Lindbergh: When I was a boy, I made up my mind that I was going to be six feet and three inches tall, and I made it with a half inch to spare.

TAKE NOTE—Two hundred thousand people greeted Lindbergh in Paris in 1927. When he arrived back in New York City, four million greeted him with a ticker-tape parade.

TRIVIA QUIZ—What woke up Lindbergh when he fell asleep during the flight? (Answer No. 83)

> *Courage is doing what you're afraid to do. There can be no courage unless you're scared.*
> —EDDIE RICKENBACKER (*survived a plane crash at sea*)

Stalag 17
War/Drama 1953

Director: Billy Wilder

Starring: William Holden, Don Taylor, Peter Graves,
Neville Brand

● ●

STORY CONCEPT—World War II airmen who fail an attempt to escape from a German prison camp realize that there's a traitor among them. They are suspicious of one person who trades goods with the guards.

THEME—First impressions are not always accurate.

FAVORITE SCENE—Price (Graves), the spy, is exposed when he fails the question about the time of day Pearl Harbor was bombed. He misses it by several hours because he was living in Berlin, which is in a different time zone, when the bomb was dropped.

MEMORABLE LINES—Price expresses disdain for Sefton (Holden).

Price: I don't like you and I never will.
Sefton: That's what some people say and the next thing you know they're married.

TAKE NOTE—William Holden, eager for his fans to like him, pleaded with Director Wilder to let his character have just one line to show that he really hated the Nazis. Wilder refused. Holden won the Best Actor award.

TRIVIA QUIZ—Where does the war hero, Dunbar (Taylor), hide in the concentration camp from the Germans? (Answer No. 84)

> *Those who talk about others will eventually be caught in their own 'mouth trap'.* —ANONYMOUS

The Stratton Story

Sports/Biography 1949

Director: Sam Wood

Starring: James Stewart, June Allyson, Agnes Moorehead, Frank Morgan

● ●

STORY CONCEPT—A Texas pitcher for the Chicago White Sox loses a leg in a hunting accident but manages a comeback with an artificial limb.

THEME—Everyone needs a crutch in life, be it God, a good man or woman, or a piece of wood.

FAVORITE SCENE—Soon after his return to the professional league, Monty Stratton (Stewart) tries to field a bunt and falls down. The runner makes it safely to first base. Seeing this as a weak spot for Monty, the next batter bunts as well, but this time Monty comes off the mound more quickly and throws the runner out.

MEMORABLE LINES—Monty proposes to Ethel (Allyson).

Monty: I've been thinking about what to get you for your birthday next week.
Ethel: What did you get?
Monty: I'm afraid you won't like it.
Ethel: What is it?
Monty: Me!

TAKE NOTE—The real Stratton was technical advisor on the film. In 1946, he won 18 games in the Texas League and was honored as the nation's Most Courageous Athlete.

TRIVIA QUIZ—What is Monty doing when he goes out at night on several so-called press interviews? (Answer No. 85)

> *You gotta be a man to play baseball for a living but you gotta have a lot of little boy in you, too. —ROY CAMPANELLA, catcher for the Brooklyn Dodgers, who was in an auto accident that disabled him for life.*

The Talk of the Town

Romantic Comedy 1942

Director: George Stevens

Starring: Jean Arthur, Cary Grant, Ronald Coleman, Edgar Buchanan

• •

STORY CONCEPT—A political activist, in trouble with the law, and a law professor fall in love with a schoolteacher whose house becomes a hideaway for the fugitive and a summer rental for the professor. The two unlikely "guests" become friends.

THEME—Honesty and open discussion pave the way for understanding.

FAVORITE SCENE—Nora Shelley (Arthur) has prepared breakfast for Professor Lightcap (Coleman). The morning's newspaper, which he's about to read, has Leopold Dilg's (Grant) picture on the front page. Seeing this, Nora screams and grabs his plate full of eggs, spilling them onto the photo of Dilg. The professor looks on in dismay as she cries out that it's not his morning for eggs, since he eats eggs only every other day.

MEMORABLE LINES—Nora questions Leopold in the attic where he's hiding.

Nora: . . . Any kind of squabble and you were always right in the middle of it. What's wrong with you, anyway?
Leopold: Well, it's a form of expression. Some people write books. Some people write music. I make speeches on street corners.

TAKE NOTE—The director shot two endings and then made the choice as to who would marry Arthur—Grant or Coleman.

TRIVIA QUIZ—Why do bloodhounds chase Professor Lightcap? (Answer No. 86)

> *Those who never retract their opinions love themselves more than they love truth.* —JOSEPH JOUBERT

Teacher's Pet
Romantic Comedy 1958

Director: George Seaton

Starring: Clark Gable, Doris Day, Gig Young,
Mamie Van Doren

● ●

STORY CONCEPT—A tough newspaper editor believes in the "university of hard knocks" type of education until he comes in contact with an attractive professor of journalism.

THEME—We all have something to learn from others, regardless of our backgrounds.

FAVORITE SCENE—City Editor James Gannon (Gable) gets competitive with Dr. Hugo Pine (Young) at a nightclub. Pine proves superior in dancing, discussing baseball, and playing the bongo drums. Gannon's achievement is that he outdrinks Pine—but only by bribing the waiter to doctor up his opponent's drinks.

MEMORABLE LINES—Gannon poses as a student and sits in on Stone's (Day) journalism class.

Erica Stone: The first rule of writing a news story; Kipling said it quite well in a poem he wrote. "I keep six honest serving men, they taught me all I knew. . ."
Gannon (interrupts): Their names are what and why and when, how and where and who—and it wasn't' Kipling. It was Emerson.
Erica Stone: No, it was Kipling. (Gannon interrupts again and she throws him out of the classroom.)

TAKE NOTE—On the set, Clark Gable chose to mingle, not with the big shots, but with the hired hands, extras, and guards. He never forgot that he was once the low man on the totem pole.

TRIVIA QUIZ—What causes Erika Stone to stagger and fall during the film? (Answer No. 87)

> *There are some things more painful than truth, but I can't think of them.* —ANONYMOUS

Three Came Home

Drama/War 1950

Director: Jean Negulesco

Starring: Claudette Colbert, Sessue Hayakawa, Patrick Knowles

●●●●●●●●●●●●●●●●●●●●●●●●●●●●●●●●●●●●●●

STORY CONCEPT—The true story of the Keiths who were imprisoned in separate camps by the Japanese during World War II, and how they survived four years of torture and humiliation.

THEME—The love for family creates a hope that endures.

FAVORITE SCENE—Agnes Newton Keith (Colbert) gets a note from her husband, Harry (Knowles), asking her to sneak out during the night to meet him at a designated spot. He arrives and they embrace before she rushes back to the camp, making it in the nick of time as the guards enter to check their sleeping quarters.

MEMORABLE LINES—The Colonel (Hayakawa) admires Mrs. Keith's writings and invites her for a talk at the end of the war.

Colonel: It is very strange to sit here and think I'll never see you again. I felt you would understand. I have no more family. My hometown was bombed.
Agnes: Where, Tokyo?
Colonel: No, Hiroshima.
Agnes: I wish there were something I could say to offer comfort. Whatever the rest is, there is no difference in our hearts for our children.

TAKE NOTE—Agnes Newton Keith, a Californian, wrote a book on Japan before the war. It was entitled *Land Below the Wind*. The movie, *Three Came Home*, is based on a later autobiography.

TRIVIA QUIZ—What famous actor starred with Colbert in *It Happened One Night*? (Answer No. 88)

Courage is fear holding on a minute longer.

—GENERAL GEORGE S. PATTON

3:10 to Yuma

Western 1957

Director: Delmer Daves

Starring: Van Heflin, Glenn Ford, Leora Dana, Felicia Farr, Henry Jones, Richard Jaeckel

• •

STORY CONCEPT—An outlaw leader, Ben Wade (Ford), is captured but his gang is still on the prowl. Drought-stricken rancher Dan Evans (Heflin) needs money and is persuaded to escort Wade in secret to a nearby town with a railway station, where they will board the train to stand trial in Yuma.

THEME—People of low standing sometimes have the highest principles.

FAVORITE SCENE—Wade and Evans get an upstairs room in the hotel where they wait for the train. Wade's gang arrives in town and Wade appears confident they will rescue him. Evans' friend, Alex Potter (Jones), the town drunk and the only one with courage to help him, is shot by the gang on the street. Wade attempts to psyche out Evans and offers him large sums of money. The pressure mounts as the minutes pass. How can he safely get them to the train?

MEMORABLE LINES—The marshal to a reluctant posse on guarding the outlaw, Wade: "Safe? Who knows what's safe? I knew a man who died looking at his wife. My own grandmother fought Indians for sixty years and choked to death on lemon pie!"

TAKE NOTE—Glenn Ford was offered the role of the rancher, but chose to play the outlaw instead.

TRIVIA QUIZ—What is the serendipity Evans and his family receive at the end of the movie? (Answer No. 89)

Courage is being scared to death, but saddling up anyway.

—JOHN WAYNE

The Tin Star

Western/Romance 1957

Director: Anthony Mann

Starring: Henry Fonda, Tony Perkins, Betsy Palmer,
John McIntire, Michel Ray, Mary Webster

● ●

STORY CONCEPT—A novice sheriff finds unexpected help from a despised bounty hunter who was once a sheriff himself. The unwanted scoundrel finds there are things more important than money when he rents the only room in town available to him from a young widow and her Indian son.

FAVORITE SCENE—Sheriff Ben Owens (Perkins) confronts the bounty hunter, Morg Hickman (Fonda), about his past life as a sheriff. Hickman reveals that his small salary as a sheriff cost the life of his wife, who needed an operation, and his newborn son.

MEMORABLE LINES—Hickman marvels at how inept young Owens is in dealing with people and firearms.

Hickman: How come they picked you (to be sheriff)?
Owens: I'm only temporary.
Hickman: You're more temporary than you think.

TAKE NOTE—Director Anthony Mann directed many westerns. Among them were *Winchester '73, Bend of the River, The Far Country, The Man from Laramie,* and *The Naked Spur.* All of them starred James Stewart.

TRIVIA QUIZ—What expensive gift does Hickman give young Kip Mayfield (Ray) when he first plans to leave town? (Answer No. 90)

> God never meant for your past to be a lock on the door of opportunity. —GYNNATH FORD

To Catch a Thief
Romance/Thriller 1955

Director: Alfred Hitchcock

Starring: Cary Grant, Grace Kelly, Brigitte Auber,
Jessie Royse Landis, John Williams

• •

STORY CONCEPT—A jewel thief is on the prowl in the French Riviera. A retired cat burglar is suspect number one. His attempt to catch the thief introduces him to a wealthy widow and her daughter, and they assist him in apprehending the thief.

THEME—A man's crooked past speaks more loudly than his present path of reform.

FAVORITE SCENE—John Robie (Grant) and Francis (Kelly) are alone in her plush suite overlooking the Riviera. Her beauty, wit, and expensive diamond necklace draw Robie close to her on the couch. The fireworks display in the background matches only the passion between the lovers. This is one of the sexiest scenes in movie history—and without nudity or heavy breathing.

MEMORABLE LINES—Jessie Stevens (Landis), impressed with Robie, quizzes him on her daughter, Francis.

Jessie: Why haven't you made a pass at my daughter?
Robie: Very pretty, quietly attractive.
Jessie: Sorry I sent her to that finishing school. I think they finished her.

TAKE NOTE—Grace Kelly met her future husband, Prince Ranier, while filming in Monte Carlo. She became Princess Grace shortly thereafter. The picture, shot in color, won Best Cinematography. Breathtaking!

TRIVIA QUIZ—What humorous lines by Kelly bring a look of dismay to Grant when they kiss at his villa in the last scene of the movie? (Answer No. 91)

The past is a guidepost, not a hitching post.

—L. THOMAS HOLDCROFT

Tomorrow Is Forever

Drama/Romance 1946

Director: Irving Pichel

Starring: Claudette Colbert, Orson Welles, George Brents, Richard Long, Natalie Wood

● ●

STORY CONCEPT—During World War I, a wife gets word that her husband was killed in action. Twenty years later he comes back to the States, disfigured, with a new identity and an adopted daughter. His boss turns out to be his wife's new husband, and he learns that he has a twenty-year-old son. He is now faced with the dilemma to tell all or keep his secret.

FAVORITE SCENE—Eric Kessler (Welles) is seen by his former wife, Elizabeth Hamilton (Colbert), as he looks at the house where they lived together over 20 years ago. She questions him about why he's there and begins to suspect that he might be her first husband.

MEMORABLE LINES—Drew (Long), unaware that Kessler is his real father, talks of peace.

Drew: Am I boring you?
Kessler: Boring me? That's the last thing you could ever do.
Drew (reading from Thomas Paine): If there must be trouble, let it be in my day, that my child might have peace.
Kessler: If I had a son, that would be my prayer each day.

TAKE NOTE—Orson Welles was bored with his role in this film because he didn't also get to produce and direct it, as he was accustomed to doing. He took the part for the money because he had spent most of his resources on getting Franklin Roosevelt elected for the fourth time.

TRIVIA QUIZ—Who appeared in her first role out of 44 in this film before mysteriously drowning at age 39? (Answer No. 92)

It is better to stumble toward a better life than not to take any steps at all. —ANONYMOUS

A Tree Grows in Brooklyn
Drama 1945

Director: Elia Kazan

Starring: Dorothy McGuire, James Dunn, Peggy Ann Garner, Joan Blondell, Lloyd Nolan, Ruth Nelson

● ●

STORY CONCEPT—A thirteen-year-old girl builds a life amidst big city poverty and an alcoholic father. When he dies and her hard-working mother bears another child, the girl takes a job in a saloon and earns the money to finish high school.

THEME—A dysfunctional family and poor environment do not prohibit a person from fulfilling his or her dreams.

FAVORITE SCENE—Poppa (Dunn) arrives home from singing at a wedding. Even though it's late, he describes the wedding in glorious and colorful detail as his family feasts on leftovers.

MEMORABLE LINES—Miss McDonough (Nelson), Francie's (Garner) teacher, offers her a leftover piece of pie. Francie takes the pie and says she will give it to a poor neighbor.

Francie: It isn't true. I wanted it for myself.
Miss McDonough: I'm not going to punish you for having an imagination. All stories and all music came out of someone's imagination. It's dangerous unless we learn how to use it. Tell the truth and write lies. They aren't lies anymore. They become stories.

TAKE NOTE—Director Kazan selected Garner to play the part of the 13-year-old because she was 13 and plain-faced. Her father was overseas in the war and her mother was having problems. This all helped Garner to play a troubled character.

TRIVIA QUIZ—Where did the gift of flowers that Francie received at her graduation come from? (Answer No. 93)

It's not the wrappings but the gift on the inside that counts.

—ROGER CRAWFORD

The Valley of Decision

Drama/Romance 1945

Director: Tay Garnett

Starring: Greer Garson, Gregory Peck, Jessica Tandy,
Donald Crisp, Lionel Barrymore, Preston Foster,
Marsha Hunt, Gladys Cooper, Dan Duryea

● ● ● ● ● ● ● ● ● ● ● ● ● ● ● ● ● ● ▶◀ ● ● ● ● ● ● ● ● ● ● ● ● ● ● ● ● ●

STORY CONCEPT—The reading of a will brings two lovers back together after being separated for ten years by a strike in a steel mill where two killings took place.

THEME—Bitterness and stubbornness are always detrimental to progress.

FAVORITE SCENE—The Scott family is shocked when the will of their mother, Clarrisa (Cooper), the matriarch of the steel family, reveals that their former housekeeper, Mary Rafferty (Garson) is to receive one-fifth of the family fortune.

MEMORABLE LINES—William Scott (Crisp) encourages his son, Paul, to marry Louise Cain (Tandy), their next door neighbor.

Paul: I'm in love with someone else, Dad. And when the strike threats are over, I'm going to England and try to bring her back. (Paul's father is dumbfounded and wonders whom he is talking about until his wife tells him that it's Mary Rafferty.)
William: Why didn't he marry her?
Clarissa: Because she wouldn't have him.

TAKE NOTE—Peck said that every time he was in a scene with Garson, her face was lit up like a lovely moon floating and that he was the dim figure beside her in the shadows. But he didn't mind because she was so beautiful.

TRIVIA QUIZ—What shocks the steel-working family of Mary Rafferty? (Answer No. 94)

> *The greatest difficulty with the world is not its inability to produce, but its unwillingness to share.* —ROY L. SMITH

Vertigo

Thriller 1958

Director: Alfred Hitchcock

Starring: Jimmy Stewart, Kim Novak, Barbara Bel Geddes

● ●

STORY CONCEPT—A detective, forced to retire because of his fear of heights, is hired to shadow the wife of a former captain on the force. He saves her from drowning and falls in love with her. She is very confused and attempts suicide again, this time successfully. He has a nervous breakdown and is obsessed with the memory of her. One day he meets a stranger on the street who looks amazingly like her. He becomes acquainted with the stranger and proceeds to mold her in the image of his former love, which ends in tragic failure.

THEME—People who want to change others need to focus on the one they have the greatest influence over, themselves.

FAVORITE SCENE—Scottie Ferguson (Stewart) knocks at the door of a complete stranger (Novak) because she resembles his former love, Madelaine. Interestingly, she invites him in and his plan succeeds as she accepts his invitation to dinner.

MEMORABLE LINES—After saving Madelaine from drowning, Scottie says: "There's an old Chinese saying; once you've saved a person's life you're committed to care for them."

TAKE NOTE—The costume designer and Hitchcock worked together to give Madelaine's clothing an eerie appearance. Her trademark gray suit was chosen for its color because they thought it seemed odd for a blond woman to be wearing all gray. In 1982, 120 critics voted this movie number ten on the all-time International Critics' poll best movie list.

TRIVIA QUIZ—What does the word vertigo mean? (Answer No. 95)

Fear is the dark room where negatives are developed.
                                                                    —ANONYMOUS

Watch on the Rhine
Drama 1943

Director: Herman Shumlin

Starring: Paul Lukas, Bette Davis, Lucile Watson,
Donald Woods, George Coulouris,
Geraldine Fitzgerald, Donald Buka

● ● ● ● ● ● ● ● ● ● ● ● ● ● ● ● ● ● ● ●▌●▐● ● ● ● ● ● ● ● ● ● ● ● ● ● ● ●

STORY CONCEPT—After eighteen years in Europe working underground against the fascists, the Kurt Muller family returns to America and find themselves faced with the enemy once again.

THEME—Freedom is not a question of doing what we like, but being able to do what we ought.

FAVORITE SCENE—Count de Brancois (Coulouris), a Nazi, discovers the true identity of freedom fighter Kurt Muller (Lukas) in the home where he is staying. To keep quiet about it, he blackmails Muller.

MEMORABLE LINES—Fanny Farrelly (Watson) sees her daughter, Sara (Davis), for the first time in eighteen years.

Fanny: You're not young anymore.
Sara: Mother, I'm thirty-eight!

TAKE NOTE—Bette Davis, different from her norm, plays a secondary role as a submissive wife who lets her husband take the lead.

TRIVIA QUIZ—Toward the end of the movie, what does the oldest Muller son, Joshua (Buka), plan to do? (Answer No. 96)

They that give up essential liberty to obtain a little temporary safety deserve neither liberty nor safety.

—BENJAMIN FRANKLIN

The Wrong Man

Drama 1956

Director: Alfred Hitchcock

Starring: Henry Fonda, Vera Miles, Anthony Quayle, Nehemiah Personoff

● ●

STORY CONCEPT —True story of a New York City musician who is mistakenly identified as a robber. The musician's wife has a nervous breakdown and is hospitalized during his trial. Even though ultimately he's acquitted, his wife remains in the mental hospital.

THEME—There's a thin line between truth and fiction, which can strike terror in the heart of the innocent.

FAVORITE SCENE—Manny (Fonda) comes home from work in the wee hours of the morning and finds his wife, Rose (Miles), fully clothed, in a chair beside the bed. He reaches out to touch her and she hits him with a hairbrush, which glances off and breaks the mirror. Manny realizes his wife is ill and takes her to the hospital.

MEMORABLE LINES—Manny, to his oldest son, Bob: "I hope you never have to go through what I've gone through. If you do, I hope you have a son to come home to just like I do."

TAKE NOTE—Hitchcock used some of the actual witnesses as actors in the film. Two years after this incident, Rose Balstrero left the hospital, and her family moved to Florida.

TRIVIA QUIZ—What further convicts Manny during a police handwriting test? (Answer No. 97)

> *Truth is always strong, no matter how weak it looks, and falsehood is always weak, no matter how strong it looks.*
> —MARCUS ANTONIUS

Yankee Doodle Dandy

Biography 1942

Director: Michael Curtiz

Starring: James Cagney, Joan Leslie, Walter Huston, Irene Manning, Jean Cagney

• •

STORY CONCEPT—The life and times of George M. Cohen, great composer, song writer, and entertainer told in flashback with Cohen going to the White House to see President Franklin D. Roosevelt, then retelling the story of his life.

THEME—Life's greatest joy comes from lifting up others.

FAVORITE SCENE—George's (Cagney's) parents are retiring from show business and a surprise birthday party for his father (Huston) takes place. George's gift is a smoking jacket with a letter in the pocket. It is meant to be read in privacy but his father insists on reading it aloud. The heartfelt letter wishes God's blessings on his father and gives thanks for his parent's love. While reading the letter, George's father becomes so emotional he has to stop.

MEMORABLE LINES—George, on several different occasions after the family performance: "My mother thanks you. My father thanks you. My sister thanks you. And I thank you."

TAKE NOTE—William Cagney, James Cagney's brother, planted the seed in Mr. Cohen's mind for his brother to play this part because Jimmy had been branded by a few as being a communist sympathizer, and he felt this movie would display his true colors of patriotism. Cagney's sister in real life plays his sister, Jean, in the movie. For his patriotic songs, George M. Cohen was awarded the Congressional Medal of Honor by President Roosevelt.

TRIVIA QUIZ—What famous holiday is George Michael Cohen born on? (Answer No. 98)

> *When someone does something good, applaud! You will make two people happy.* —SAMUEL GOLDWYN

The Yearling

Drama 1946

Director: Clarence Brown

Starring: Gregory Peck, Jane Wyman, Claude Jarman, Jr., Forrest Tucker, Chill Wills

• •

STORY CONCEPT—A young boy growing up in the Florida wilderness wants a baby deer as a pet. The deer is good news for him but bad news for the crops that the animal devours. The solution to the problem brings maturity to the boy.

THEME—Becoming an adult means losing a part of oneself and gaining another.

FAVORITE SCENE—Jody (Jarman) explains to his father (Peck) that the reason his mother (Wyman) raves so much is because she's lost three small children and she doesn't want to lose another one.

MEMORABLE LINES—After six days of rain and Ma's complaining about having a deer in the house with rotting corn and beans, the rain stops. Pa puts his arm around her and says, "Ma, seems like times a body gets struck down so low ain't a power on earth can ever bring him up again. . . . seems like something inside him dies so he don't want to get up again, but he does. Ain't much of a world left for us, but that's all we got. Let's be thankful we got a world at all."

TAKE NOTE—One scene with the fawn took 72 takes because she kept running away from the heat of the studio lights.

TRIVIA QUIZ—Who gave the name Flag to the fawn and why? (Answer No. 99)

> *Anyone who limits her vision to memories of yesterday is already dead.* —LILY LANGTRY

The Young Philadelphians
Drama/Romance 1959

Director: Victor Sherman

Starring: Paul Newman, Barbara Rush, Alexis Smith,
Brian Keith, Robert Vaughn, Diane Brewster,
Billie Burke

● ●

STORY CONCEPT—A young lawyer, climbing the social ladder, loses his fiancée to a wealthy competitor and decides to make it to the top himself, regardless of the price.

THEME—The path to success is rough when you take short cuts that are questionable.

FAVORITE SCENE—Lawyer Tony Lawrence (Newman) has decided to defend his friend, Chester Gwynn (Vaughn) when he learns that his fiancée, Joan (Rush), has visited Gwynn in jail and urged him to get someone else to defend him. She fears Tony will be embarrassed in his efforts because he's not a trial lawyer. Enraged by her lack of trust in him, Tony breaks off the engagement.

MEMORABLE LINES—Tony and Joan after he's accepted a rival firm's offer of more money:

Joan: No one could blame you for taking the better offer.
Tony (alluding to her marriage to a man of wealth): We all do that in the long run, don't we?

TAKE NOTE—Four months after this film completed shooting, Newman paid off his studio contract to the tune of $500,000. He was getting $17,500 per picture at the time.

TRIVIA QUIZ—What was Joan's response when Tony asked her out for a hamburger on their first date? (Answer No. 100)

A man without decision can never be said to belong to himself....
He belongs to whatever can make captive of him.

—JOHN FOSTER

TRIVIA QUIZ Answers

1. The African Queen.
2. Pheasant.
3. Irresistible impulse.
4. He gave her respect.
5. Jonathan Shields, the producer, wanted to make another movie with them.
6. He sees Korean orphans looking for food in the airbase garbage.
7. His face is never shown.
8. He had been in the Air Force for 3½ years and had some understanding of the problems of readjusting to civilian life.
9. *The Preacher's Wife* directed by Penny Marshall.
10. "Rock Around the Clock."
11. Grandpa on "The Waltons."
12. He breaks the Comanche lance.
13. It's the phone number of Wiecek's mother.
14. Ronald Reagan.
15. Rosebud.
16. Marlon Brando for *On the Waterfront*.
17. Joan Fontaine, her sister.
18. His case was identical to her father's case.
19. From the name Carpenter and the way in which he is violently killed and resurrected.
20. Talkies replaced silent films, and Fredric March had a great voice.
21. A radio and a cake.
22. Cain and Abel, the sons of Adam who once lived in the Garden of Eden.
23. Winston Churchill.
24. "There's nothing so trustworthy as the ordinary mind of the ordinary people."
25. Be natural.
26. Boston Red Sox.

27. Brothers must serve duty on separate ships.

28. The golfers play first in sunny California, Arizona, and Florida. Then they head north when the sun is shining.

29. California's High Sierra Mountains.

30. Pat Boone.

31. Flickering lights and mysterious noises.

32. A gentleman's agreement is an unwritten code that exists. (i.e. not to rent to Jews or Blacks).

33. Oil.

34. The U.S. military units were not integrated until after World War II.

35. *The Bells of St. Mary.*

36. She looks in her keepsake box, takes out a piggy bank and some earrings, and then burns the cards and letters.

37. "Wherever I go, wherever I may be, you will always be in my heart, dear Mr. Allison — always."

38. The famous Lassie.

39. "Leaning on the Everlasting Arms" by E.A. Hoffman.

40. Mahalia Jackson.

41. The guests and staff all sleep together on a raised floor near the stove.

42. By reading classic literature aloud to the Dorn family.

43. Clarence Oddbody.

44. Listen to God and talk to a preacher.

45. Burt Lancaster, at age 37.

46. Actor Ronald Reagan.

47. When Rocco tells her he's leaving her behind, she throws herself at him, weeping, and takes the gun from his pocket, which she then slips to McCloud.

48. *The Keys of the Kingdom.*

49. Edgar Rice Burroughs' *Tarzan* series.

50. "Where's the rest of me?"

51. Nettie (Gray), his former neighbor and babysitter.

52. The abuses in the medical field, including those of the pharmaceutical companies.
53. In a grandfather clock in Laura's apartment.
54. Lora May Finney.
55. There is no score, only the sounds of the sea.
56. He can't swim.
57. Will Varner (Welles), her authoritative father.
58. *The Hunchback of Notre Dame* and *The Phantom of the Opera*.
59. She felt threatened that Clara would take her place in Marty's life.
60. The postal service delivers all of the letters addressed to Santa to the courtroom where the trial is being conducted.
61. USS *Reluctant*.
62. To rehabilitate and marry Doc Holliday, her former love from Boston.
63. Mi's father trained Mrs. Brown to swim the English Channel.
64. She uses some of it to make paper dolls.
65. Warning messages were sent by the *Californian* but the dispatcher put them aside and tended to more mundane personal passenger messages.
66. Marry him.
67. Makes a cameo appearance.
68. Her superiors were trying to teach her humility.
69. Roller skates—the ones her father had given to Arnold because of her selfish attitude.
70. Taking back his girlfriend, Kathy Moffett.
71. "So would I."
72. She opens a clinic and school for blacks in her Mississippi hometown.
73. He throws it into the furnace of a threshing machine.
74. A key to the cottage where he and Paula lived.
75. *Rey and the High Himalayas* and *Bazaar* magazine.
76. Audrey Hepburn, Best Actress (in her first major role).
77. From the Bournemouth, England, resort where the movie was filmed and guests all sit at separate tables when dining.

78. He gobbled like a turkey.

79. Reading pulp mystery stories and trying to plan the perfect murder.

80. Soda Pop.

81. *You've Got Mail.*

82. The release of long repressed love.

83. A fly.

84. In the water tank.

85. Taking dancing lessons.

86. Because of the scent in the professor's house slippers, which Dilg has worn.

87. When James Gannon unexpectedly kisses her.

88. Clark Gable.

89. It begins to rain.

90. A horse.

91. "So this is where you live? Oh, Mother will love it up here!"

92. Natalie Wood.

93. Before his death, her father Johnny Nolan had ordered them to be delivered.

94. When she takes a job as a maid in the despised steel mill owner's house.

95. Dizziness, a feeling that things are turning around.

96. Go back to Europe to find his father and fight for freedom.

97. He makes the same spelling error that the real thief made.

98. The Fourth of July (really the third).

99. Jody's crippled friend, Fodderwing, because the tail looked like a flag.

100. I like chili.

Actors Index

Directors Index

Genre Index

Fantasy

Musicals

Romance

Science Fiction

Sports

Thriller

War

Western

About the Author

Gynnath Ford is the author of *Treasures of the Silver Screen: Remembering 20th Century Movies* and four other inspirational books. He has viewed thousands of movies over the past few decades. He is a motivational speaker who uses movies to inspire and encourage.

A Note to the Reader

Any information found in this book which is not accurate, please feel free to write to us and we will make corrections in future printings.

If you know the author of any of the quotations that do not have a source we are anxious to give credit where credit is due.

Perhaps you have a best liked movie. Send us the title and a couple of sentences as to why it's your favorite. We may include it in the next "Movie Treasures" book from Highlands Publishing! Be sure to include your name so we can give you credit.

Quick Order Form

Fax orders: (615)-385-5915. Send this form.

Telephone orders: Call 1-800-331-5991 toll free.
Have your credit card ready.

Postal orders: Highlands Publishing, Box 50021, Nashville, TN 37205

I would like to order _____ copies of *MovieTreasures of the '40s and '50s* @ $14.95 each

I would like to order _____ copies of *Treasures of the Silver Screen* @ $14.99 each

(Non-profit groups and large orders please inquire about our discount pricing.)

Name: _____

Address: _____

City: _____ **State:** _____ **Zip:** _____

Telephone: _____

E-mail: _____

Sales tax: Please add 8.25% for books shipped to Tennessee addresses.

Shipping: Air—US: $4.00 for first book and $2.00 for each additional book. Surface—US: $2.00 for the first book and $2.00 for each additional book.

International: $9.00 for the first book and $5.00 for each additional book (estimate).

Payment: ❑ Check   ❑ Credit Card: ❑ Visa   ❑ Mastercard

Card number: _____ **Exp. date:** _____

Name on card: _____